THE EYES
OF TEXAS
TRAVEL
GUIDE

San Antonio/Border Edition

THE EYES OF TEXAS

TRAVEL GUIDE

San Antonio/Border Edition

By Ray Miller

Cordovan Corporation, Publishers
Houston 1979

EYES OF TEXAS TRAVEL GUIDE
San Antonio/Border Edition
First Printing August 1979
Second Printing November 1979

Library of Congress Catalog Number: 79-90085
ISBN: 0-89123-068-8
         0-89123-069-6 pbk

Cover design: Russell Jumonville
Maps: Anita Schmoekel
Production art: Ron S. Tammariello
Research: Lorel Kane

We dedicate this book to all of the individuals and officials and institutions we have drawn on over the years for help in preparing our television program and these travel guides.

We are indebted especially to Jack Maguire and the Institute of Texan Cultures, the Texas State Library, the Texas Historical Commission, the Department of Parks and Wildlife, the Department of Highways and Public Transportation, the Houston Public Library, and Doris Glasser, the historical societies of the various counties, Nancy Crow and the Cordovan staff and the hundreds of Texans who share our appreciation for this unique state.

Ray Miller and the staff of "Eyes of Texas"
Houston, Texas
August, 1979

Contents

Foreword

The Texas Tourist Development Agency and the Texas Department of Highways and Public Transportation developed a network of Texas Travel Trails in the 1960s while I was governor of Texas. Ray Miller was an early and enthusiastic supporter of the travel trails.

His devotion to our state continues to be manifested in his television programs and in this series of "Eyes of Texas" travel guides. They have increased our awareness of the history and heritage of our state and they have helped encourage the preservation and restoration of historic buildings and historic sites.

The *Eyes of Texas Travel Guide, San Antonio/Border Edition* focuses on the part of the state where I was born. I join the author in the hope that this book will encourage you to see some more of Texas.

John B. Connally,
Governor of Texas,
1962-1968.

Introduction

This is the third book in our series of Texas travel guides. It covers most of the most Spanish part of Texas. This area was Spanish territory for more than three hundred years and most of the early Spanish settlements were near the Rio Grande and in the area around San Antonio.

We have included in this book the counties surrounding San Antonio and the counties south and west of San Antonio to the border. All of the border counties are included in this edition except Hidalgo and Cameron counties. They are included in the first volume in this series, the *Eyes of Texas Travel Guide, Gulf Coast Edition.* Some of the oldest settlements, most of the oldest missions, some of the earliest ranches, almost all of the mountains and many of the early forts are in the part of Texas covered in this edition.

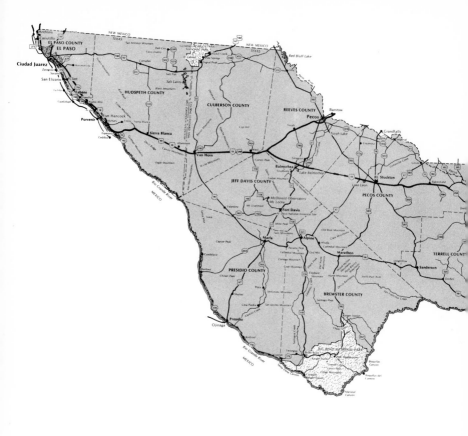

The San Antonio
and border area

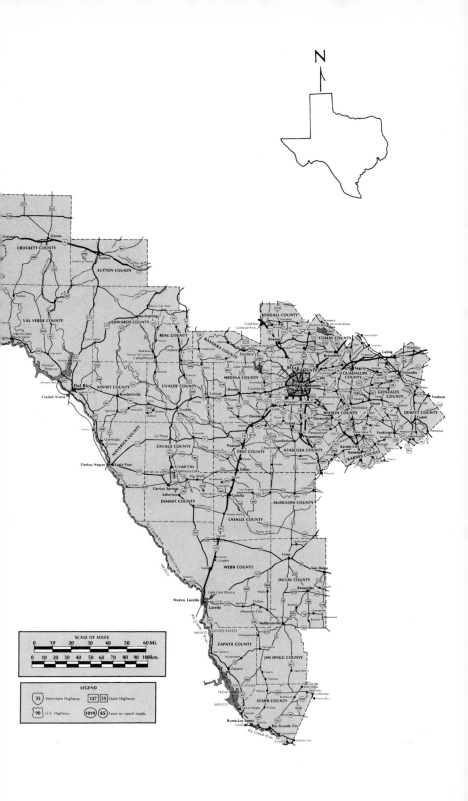

The San Antonio Area

Bexar, Wilson, Karnes, DeWitt, Gonzales,
Guadalupe, Comal, Kendall, Bandera,
Medina, Frio, Atascosa counties.

The war that made Texas independent of Mexico ended at San Jacinto, outside the present city of Houston. But the war started in the San Antonio area. The first shot was fired at Gonzales. The first disaster occurred at the Alamo in San Antonio. Some of the state's most historic places are in the San Antonio area. The finest assortment of Spanish mission architecture in the United States is here.

Some of the earliest ranches in the present United States were established here before the American Revolution by Spaniards. The word *ranch* is derived from the Spanish *rancho* and *rancher* comes from the Spanish *ranchero*. Ranches in the counties around San Antonio sent many herds up the old Chisholm Trail through Round Rock and Austin and Fort Worth in the days between the end of the Civil War and the arrival of the railroads.

Visitors to this area will need several days to see everything that deserves to be seen in San Antonio itself. It will take more than a week to see the principal points of interest in all the twelve counties we have included in this section.

You may want to stay in San Antonio and make side trips to the surrounding counties. Or you may want to see San Antonio and then make a swing around the surrounding territory through Karnes City, Cuero, Gonzales, Seguin, New Braunfels, Bandera, Hondo, Devine and Pleasanton. Such a trip would require more than one day so you will need to pick a place to stop overnight. We would choose New Braunfels.

1

The Texans occupied San Antonio and the Alamo in December of 1835 and remained in control until President Santa Anna of Mexico recaptured the Alamo on March 6, 1836. All the defending Texans were slain. The Alamo was badly damaged in the fighting. Only the chapel and some of the walls of a few other buildings of the original mission survived. The U.S. Army put the chapel back together in the 1840s and used it as a quartermaster depot for a while.

BEXAR COUNTY

San Antonio is one of America's great cities. Many people regard it as the most beautiful city in Texas. It is certainly the most historic.

There never was any question here, as there was in many other counties, about which city would be the county seat. San Antonio was the only city ever considered. The present courthouse was built in 1891. This city has been fought over more than any other city in Texas, and it has changed hands more times than any other city in Texas.

Mexican revolutionaries seized the city from the Spanish authorities in 1811. The Spanish took it back, but lost it again in 1813 to some Mexican revolutionaries supported by American adventurers. The Spanish recaptured it and held it until they lost the whole territory to the Mexican revolutionaries in 1821. Texas revolutionaries led by Ben Milam captured San Antonio from the Mexicans in December of

A merchant named Honore Grenet bought the Alamo site in 1878 and he built a big bazaar here with a facade designed to resemble a fort. Another businessman was threatening to buy it and build a hotel. That alarmed the Daughters of the Republic. They petitioned the state to buy the property, but the legislature was not in session. So Clara Driscoll of the DRT bought the property and held it until the state was able to acquire it. Workmen demolishing the emporium Grenet had built discovered some of the original Spanish walls and foundations and the restoration began in 1912.

1835. Milam was killed in the fighting, but his troops forced Mexican General Martín Perfecto de Cos to surrender and abandon the city. This caused the Mexican president Antonio Lopez de Santa Anna to bring a major invasion force into Texas to crush the revolution. He laid siege to the Alamo and finally captured it on March 6, 1836. The Mexican leader had decreed there would be no quarter, and most accounts say the entire Texas garrison commanded by William B. Travis died fighting. The Mexican army left San Antonio after Santa Anna was defeated by Sam Houston at San Jacinto. But Mexican expeditions seized the town briefly on two occasions in 1842. Confederate soldiers forced the Union garrison to surrender the town in 1861 and then the Confederates handed it back again in 1866. That was the last time San Antonio changed hands. There are historical markers all over the area commemorating the events that have punctuated the history of this area.

This is one of the original counties, organized in 1836 immediately after Texas won its independence from Mexico. The area had been a municipality with the same name under the Spanish and Mexican rule. The name is the one the Spanish applied to the first presidio they established here in 1718. The father of the Spanish viceroy ruling Mexico at the time was the Duke de Bexar. The original Bexar District ex-

3

1) Ben Milam was a native of Kentucky. He came to Texas in 1818. Milam was killed in the fighting at San Antonio and he is buried in the Ben Milam Square here. 2) The Spanish colonial building at 105 Military Plaza in downtown San Antonio is known as the Spanish Governors' Palace.

1

tended all the way to the Panhandle. Dozens of other counties were formed from the original county of Bexar over the years.

Martin Alarcon established the first mission and the first presidio here. He named the mission San Antonio de Valero, and it came to be known as the Alamo. The presidio Alarcon founded to protect the Alamo was named San Antonio de Bexar.

The missions Concepcion, Espada, San Jose and San Juan Capistrano were developed along the San Antonio River in the early eighteenth century. The Spanish brought in some settlers from the Canary Islands in 1731 to establish a civil colony.

The settlement took the name of the presidio, and San Antonio de Bexar became the headquarters of the Spanish administration in Texas in 1772. For a long time, the captain of the garrison at San Antonio de Bexar was also the governor of the territory. The captain lived in a townhouse built in 1749

Antonio Lopez de Santa Anna was in his forties when he led the Mexican army north into Texas in 1836 to put an end to the revolution. He had been a soldier for 25 years. Santa Anna rose to national prominence by adroitly switching sides at crucial points in the various revolutions and uprisings, after he joined the Spanish army as a teenager. He was very popular with the Mexican public. He was handsome and he had a flashy personality that made his constituents overlook the casual brutality he displayed toward the defenders of the Alamo and the prisoners at Goliad. He returned to Mexico in disgrace after Sam Houston defeated him at San Jacinto, but Santa Anna regained his popularity. He was head of the Mexican government again by 1841, and he was a factor in Mexican political affairs until he died in 1876 at the age of 82.

at 105 Military Plaza. This came to be known as the Governors' Palace. It is preserved and open to visitors every day. There is a small fee. It is now known as the Spanish Governors' Palace, and it is listed in the *National Register of Historic Places.* Twenty-seven other sites in the San Antonio area are listed in the register. Only Travis County has more.

The Alamo is open to visitors every day except Christmas Eve and Christmas Day. There is no fee. The old mission where Travis and his men perished is on Alamo Plaza in the heart of the city. The ruined mission was claimed by the Republic of Texas, the Catholic Church and the U.S. Government at various times. The state bought the church's interest out in 1883 and put the Alamo in the custody of the city of San Antonio. It was later transferred to the custody of the Daughters of the Republic of Texas.

All four of the old missions on the south side of San Antonio are still serving as Catholic churches. San Jose at 6539 San Jose Drive is also a state park and a national historic site. It has often been described as the finest Spanish mission in North America. San Jose is open to visitors every day. There is a small admission fee. The Mission Nuestra Senora de la Purisima Concepcion at 807 Mission Road, the Mission San Francisco de la Espada on Espada Road off U.S. Highway 281, and the Mission San Juan Capistrano at 9101 Graf Street all are open to visitors every day for a small fee.

1

1) *The Mission San Jose'y San Miguel de Aguayo has been described as the most elegant Spanish mission building in Texas and some consider it the finest mission in North America. San Jose'was founded in 1720. The present building was built of limestone from a nearby quarry sometime after 1727. The building was neglected after 1800, but it has now been restored. 2) The famous "Rose Window" somehow escaped damage and vandalism and it survives as a testimonial to the craftsmanship of Pedro Huizar. 3) The Mission Nuestra Senora de la Purisima Concepcion de Acuna was established in East Texas in 1716. It was moved to San Antonio in 1731. The present building probably was not completed until the 1760s.*

2

3

1) The missions San Francisco de la Espada and 2) San Juan Capistrano were built a little farther from San Antonio than the missions Concepcion and San Jose. Espada and Capistrano both were moved here from East Texas, as Concepcion was in 1731. All four missions pictured here will be included in the San Antonio Missions National Historic Park now being developed. They are all open to visitors every day for a small fee.

All the old missions here are listed in the *National Register of Historic Places.* The National Park Service is now developing a San Antonio Missions National Historic Park to include these four missions and the adjoining land and the old

1

1) *The Spanish built all their missions here near the San Antonio River and they developed a network of* aqueducts they called acequias *to carry water from the river to their compounds and their fields. 2) A museum and a number of unusual shops are features of La Villita today. President Santa Anna stayed here while his troops besieged the Alamo. He got interested in a young San Antonio woman and asked her to marry him. He was already married, but he got one of his soldiers to dress up as a priest and they fooled the lady with a phony ceremony. This lady was not in Santa Anna's tent at the battle of San Jacinto. That was another lady.*

2

aqueduct the Spanish missionaries built to carry water to the Mission Espada.

The people of San Antonio have not been as anxious to tear down their old buildings as the citizens of some of our other major cities have been. So there is something left here, still, of the little village that was here in the early days when the battles were being fought around the Alamo. La Villita goes back to the early eighteenth century, and it was in ruins in 1939 when Mayor Maury Maverick Sr. and architect O'Neil Ford started restoring it. Today La Villita is one of the beauty spots on the San Antonio River in downtown San Antonio.

A marker on the building at 503 Villita testifies that the Mexican General Martín Perfecto de Cos signed here in 1835 that agreement to surrender the Alamo to the Texas revolutionaries. The building is called the Cos House. Cos promised in the articles of surrender that he would take his Mexican troops back south of the Rio Grande and stay out of any future fighting between Texans and Mexicans. Cos was back

1) One of the restored buildings in La Villita is the house where the Mexican general Martin Perfecto de Cos signed the agreement surrendering San Antonio and the Alamo to the Texas revolutionaries in December of 1835. 2) Cos promised to go back to Mexico and stay out of any future fighting, but Santa Anna canceled that promise. He brought Cos back with him when he came to San Antonio to recapture the Alamo in March of 1836.

2

again two months later, though, trying again to put down the Texas Revolution. He probably did not have a lot of choice. The Mexican president Santa Anna was Cos' brother-in-law, and Santa Anna was just not the kind of fellow to whom a brother-in-law could say, "I cannot go back and fight Texans any more because I promised not to." Santa Anna stayed here in La Villita while his troops were besieging the Alamo from February 24 to March 6 of 1836. He and Cos won that battle, but they lost the war.

The old San Antonio Museum in Bolivar Hall in La Villita features displays about the historical events that have occurred here. The museum is open daily except Mondays. There is no admission fee, but donations are encouraged. The address is 511 Villita Street.

There are outdoor musical presentations in the Arneson River Theater in La Villita on Tuesday, Friday and Saturday nights during the Fiesta Noche del Rio, from June through August.

A river walk follows the San Antonio River for several blocks in downtown San Antonio, past hotels, shops,

1) Architect Robert Hugman designed a river walk with bridges and stairways to beautify the downtown section of the San Antonio River in the 1930s. The river walk has become one of the city's principal attractions. 2) José Antonio Navarro lived and practiced law in a complex of three stone and adobe buildings at the corner of Nuevo and Laredo streets. He died here in 1871 and people say the ghosts of Navarro and a couple of people murdered here after his time still haunt the buildings.

restaurants and historic sites. There is nothing remotely like this anywhere else in Texas.

Some of the relics of San Antonio's more recent past have also been preserved. The State Department of Parks and Wildlife is restoring the old home and office used by José Antonio Navarro in the 1850s. The buildings are at Laredo and Nuevo. They are stuccoed limestone and well preserved. Navarro was a member of a prominent Spanish family. He sided with the Mexicans against Spain and then sided with the Texans against Mexico. He and one of his relatives were the only native-born Texans to sign the Texas Declaration of Independence. Navarro was prominent in politics after the

1) The Bexar County Courthouse was completed in 1896. 2) The Yturri-Edmunds Home at 257 Yellowstone is owned by the San Antonio Conservation Society and the home and the old mill on the same property are open to visitors. The land the buildings occupy was part of the original Mission Concepción property. It was granted to the Yturri family by the Republic of Mexico in 1824. The house dates from about 1840. The mill was built earlier, but it is no longer in its original form. 3) The Catholic Order of Ursuline Sisters built a school for girls on the San Antonio River in the 1850s. A hundred years later, the Ursuline Academy moved to a new location and the original Ursuline Academy became the Southwest Craft Center.

revolution, and Navarro County was named for him. There will be a small fee when the Navarro place is opened to visitors.

The old Yturri-Edmunds Home and mill at 257 Yellowstone are open to visitors Tuesdays through Saturdays. There is no admission charge here.

An old rock house where O. Henry once lived has been moved to the grounds of the Lone Star Brewery and set up as a museum. The house is at 600 Lone Star Boulevard, and it is open every day except Thanksgiving, Christmas and New Year's. The brewery also has a vast display of horns and antlers and stuffed animals and birds in the Buckhorn Hall of Horns on the brewery grounds. This also is open every day

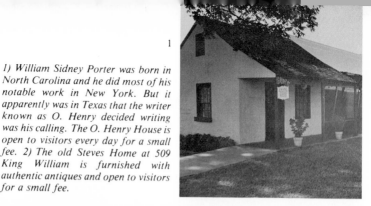

1) William Sidney Porter was born in North Carolina and he did most of his notable work in New York. But it apparently was in Texas that the writer known as O. Henry decided writing was his calling. The O. Henry House is open to visitors every day for a small fee. 2) The old Steves Home at 509 King William is furnished with authentic antiques and open to visitors for a small fee.

except Thanksgiving, Christmas and New Year's. There are admission fees at each of the museums on the brewery grounds.

The Lone Star Brewery at 600 Lone Star Boulevard is the place where Lone Star beer is made and bottled, but there is another building also known as the Lone Star Brewery. The other one is on Jones Avenue. The brewery on Jones Avenue was built in 1884. Several brands of beer were made here. None carried the Lone Star label, but the name of the company was Lone Star Brewing. The brewery on Jones Avenue closed in 1915. The building is being renovated now to house the San Antonio Museum of Art.

Some of the prosperous pioneers here built imposing homes on King William Street in the 1800s, and some of the homes

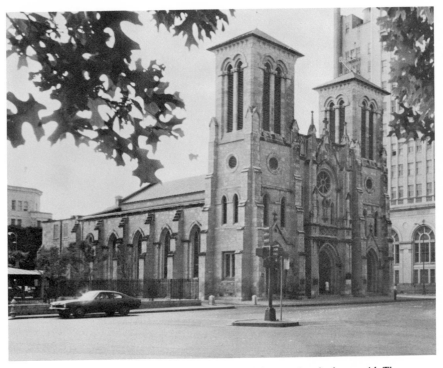

San Fernando Cathedral on Main Plaza is more than two hundred years old. The Canary Islanders the Spanish brought here laid the foundation for this church in 1738. The original building was finished in 1749. Ben Milam was married here and some of the defenders of the Alamo are buried here.

are still standing. King William Street is listed in the *National Register of Historic Places*. And the old Steves Home at 509 King William is open to visitors every day, as an example of what a rich family's residence was like in San Antonio in the Victorian age. There is a small admission fee.

The San Fernando Cathedral on Main Plaza was built by the original Canary Island settlers in the 1740s. The building has been changed and remodeled and added onto a number of times over the years. Architect O'Neil Ford started an effort in 1977 to restore the old church to something like it was in the beginning. Ben Milam was married in the San Fernando Church in 1831 to Ursula Maria de Veramendi. Her father was vice-governor of Coahuila and Texas at the time. The remains of some of the Texans killed at the Alamo are buried in the cathedral.

1) *This is some of the elaborate landscaping in Brackenridge Park. The park also includes one of the finest zoos in North America. 2) The Witte Museum in Brackenridge Park is to San Antonio what the Smithsonian is to the nation. There are exhibits here on history and archaeology. There are collections of art and period furnishings, too.*

There is an unusually fine zoo in Brackenridge Park. The park is named for George Washington Brackenridge because Brackenridge gave the city the land. Brackenridge came to Texas from Indiana with his parents in the 1850s. His father ran a store during the Civil War, and he took in a lot of cotton from farmers unable to pay money for the things they needed. George Brackenridge went into business after the war selling that cotton. He did very well, went on into banking and other profitable enterprises, and became very rich. He never married; he gave much of his wealth to the University of Texas and other schools. The Witte Memorial Museum in Brackenridge Park has exhibits covering early history and archaeology. Paintings and collections of period furnishings are also on display here. The Witte Museum is open every day, and donations of fifty cents for adults and twenty-five cents for children are encouraged.

1) Robert E. Lee was commander of the army post at San Antonio before the Civil War. He was still in Texas when this state seceded from the Union. 2) The U.S. Army used rented buildings and the Alamo to shelter its forces in San Antonio until the first permanent base was built at what is now Fort Sam Houston. Work on the tower and the quadrangle began in 1876.

Pioneer Hall is another museum in Brackenridge Park. It is at 3805 Broadway. Exhibits here are mostly historical. Pioneer Hall is open every day except Monday, and there is a small admission fee.

The city of San Antonio and the United States Army have had a long and agreeable association. There was a U.S. Army post here before the Civil War. Robert E. Lee was one of the commanders of the post. Lee had been assigned to other duties, but he was still here when Texas seceded from the Union in 1861. His home state of Virginia had not seceded at the time, and so Lee was still wearing the uniform of the United States when he left Texas. The seizure of San Antonio by Texas Confederates occurred before the shooting started at Fort Sumter.

The U.S. Army returned to San Antonio after the Civil War and re-established the quartermaster depot in the Alamo and also occupied some rented buildings nearby. The city of San Antonio wanted a permanent army base established, and there was a long series of negotiations, offers of land and

NATCHEZ

1) The quadrangle at Fort Sam Houston was an Apache campground for a period in 1886. Chief Geronimo and some of his followers were confined here for a month after they surrendered to U.S. troops in Arizona. The Apaches were re-settled in Florida and then moved to Fort Sill, Oklahoma, in 1888. Geronimo was 56 when he surrendered. He was 79 when he died at Fort Sill. The Indian sitting on the ground to the right of Geronimo, with the head band, is Natchez, son of the Apache chief Cochise. 2) The story is that deer and other animals were brought here to make the Indians feel more at home. Animals still roam the quadrangle.

2

counter proposals. President U. S. Grant was siding with San Antonio by 1873, but General Philip Sheridan and General William T. Sherman both argued that the spreading network of railroads was going to make it unnecessary for the army to have a big supply depot like the one proposed for San Antonio. Sheridan eventually changed his mind, and the contract finally was let in 1876 for the first part of what became the Fort Sam Houston Quadrangle. The quadrangle is listed in the *National Register of Historic Places*. The original purpose of the base here was to supply and reinforce the forts on the frontier to the west. The enemies were the Indians, but they became less of a problem after 1886 when the Apache chief Geronimo and a band of his followers surrendered to a battalion of troops from Fort Sam Houston in Arizona. The

1) *One of the several entrances to Fort Sam Houston. The base is open and the attitude toward visitors is unusually casual for a military base.* 2) *The home the army maintains for the commanding general of the Fifth Army at Fort Sam Houston is a limestone mansion built in 1881 called the Pershing House.*

Apaches were brought to San Antonio by special train. Tents were set up for them in the quadrangle at Fort Sam and they camped here for more than a month, until the army moved them on to Florida. One story is that the army brought in some deer and other animals to make the Indians feel at home, and this is said to be how the custom of keeping deer in the quadrangle began. There are deer here still, and other assorted animals and birds, too.

The commanding general's residence at Fort Sam was built in 1881. It is called the Pershing House. General John J. Pershing was living here and commanding Fort Sam Houston when we entered World War I. He was transferred from here

1) *Kelly Air Force Base in San Antonio goes back to the days when the air force was a branch of the army. This is the oldest military air training base in the United States. 2) The Brooks Air Force Base in San Antonio is now the headquarters of the Aerospace Medical Command. The school uses a centrifuge and other devices to simulate the stresses pilots must survive.*

to command the American Expeditionary Force. Dwight Eisenhower and Carl Spaatz both were serving here as lieutenants at the time. Fort Sam Houston is northeast of downtown and there is an entrance off I-35. Fort Sam is more like a park than a fort: visitors can enter, leave and wander around freely.

Kelly Air Force Base is the oldest military air training base in the United States. The base was named for Lieutenant George S. M. Kelly, the first American pilot ever killed in a military plane. He was flying a Curtis Pusher when it crashed in May of 1911. Charles Lindbergh, Billy Mitchell and Hap Arnold all took flight training here. Kelly Air Force Base is on General Hudnell Drive in southwest San Antonio and open to visitors only by arrangement with the visitors' office at 512-925-7951.

Brooks Air Force Base was established during World War I and Hangar Number 9 at Brooks is believed to be the oldest surviving military hangar in the state of Texas. Hangar 9

1) Randolph Air Force Base is now the official records center for the air force and some training still is carried on here, too, but not as much as once was. This was Randolph Field before there was an air force. It was the chief training center for the flying officers of the Army Air Corps and it was featured in several movies made during and before World War II. 2) Camp Travis was built hurriedly to train troops during World War I.

2

houses an aviation museum named for the late astronaut Edward H. White II. The museum is open every weekday, and there are organized tours of the Aerospace Medical Center on the base the first two Fridays of each month. Brooks Air Force Base entrance is in southwest San Antonio, near the intersection of I-37 and Loop 410. The museum is open from eight to four Mondays through Fridays. Tours of the rest of the base must be arranged in advance by phoning 512-536-3234.

Lackland Air Force Base is the principal air force basic training camp. It has a museum featuring displays on the history and traditions of the air force. The museum is open daily, including Saturdays, Sundays and holidays. Lackland Air Force Base is in southwest San Antonio near the intersec-

1) The Hall of Texas History on the Hemisfair grounds features life-size dioramas depicting scenes from the state's past. It is open every day. 2) San Antonio staged a world's fair in 1968 and called it the Hemisfair. The theme building for the fair was the Tower of the Americas. It still towers over San Antonio. There is a restaurant on top and an observation deck open every day.

tion of Loop 410 and U.S. 90.

Randolph Air Force Base has become the official records center for the air force. Randolph was built in 1928, and it was known as the West Point of the Air before the Air Force Academy was built in Colorado.

Camp Travis was absorbed into Fort Sam Houston a few years after World War I, but Travis was a major training base for the army in 1917 and 1918. Hundreds of frame barracks were thrown up in a few months time. The Ninetieth Division trained here, and the Eighteenth Division was in training when the war ended.

Visitors to San Antonio will be interested in several attractions around Hemisfair Plaza where the 1968 Texas World's Fair was held.

The Tower of the Americas has an observation deck on top and dining rooms at two levels. The observation deck is open every day. There is an admission fee.

The Hall of Texas History Museum in the Hemisfair Plaza is a wax museum with exhibits depicting various incidents in the history of Texas. It is open every day. The admission fee is a dollar for adults and fifty cents for children and military personnel in uniform.

The San Antonio Museum of Transportation in the Hemisfair Plaza has a collection of vehicles including an early

1

2

3

1) There is a fine collection of old cars, carriages, trolleys and bikes in the San Antonio Museum of Transportation in Hemisfair Plaza. 2) One of the state's major assets is the Institute of Texan Cultures in Hemisfair Plaza. It is a library and research center. 3) Two Texans from the Philippines demonstrate the tinikling at the Folk Life Festival. The Festival is staged every summer by the Institute of Texan Cultures.

mule trolley car, a stagecoach, carriages and some antique automobiles. The Museum of Transportation is open daily. There is a small admission fee.

The Institute of Texan Cultures stages the Texas Folklife Festival every August. Another major event in San Antonio is the Fiesta San Antonio in April, featuring parades, concerts and dancing in the streets.

1

1) The San Antonio River Walk is decorated with lights and luminarias on a weekend before Christmas each year, for the Fiesta de las Luminarias. 2) The Menger is said to be the oldest hotel in the United States still standing in its original form. Theodore Roosevelt recruited some of the Rough Riders for his expedition to Cuba here in the Menger bar. 3) The Saint Anthony, built in 1909, is filled with art and antiques and many travelers rank it with the world's greatest hotels.

2

3

An old stagecoach inn north of San Antonio has been turned into a restaurant. This was originally a stage stop on the line between San Antonio and Kerrville. It is now called the Settlement Inn. It is in Leon Springs and the chef's specialty is barbecue.

A Christmas pageant called Los Pastores is staged at the Mission San Jose each year, on a weekend in early January. And a Christmas pageant called La Posadas is held each year on a Sunday before Christmas.

Other museums in San Antonio:

● Herzberg Circus Collection, Public Library, 210 W. Market Street, open weekdays and Sunday afternoons.

● Marion Koogler McNay Art Institute, 6000 New Braunfels Avenue. Collection of fine art displayed in the late Mrs. McNay's home. No admission charge.

Additional San Antonio sites listed in the *National Register of Historic Places:*

● Arsenal, South Flores at East Arsenal.

● Fest-Steves Buildings, 111-121 Military Plaza, nineteenth century commercial buildings.

● I.G.N. Railroad Station, Medina at Houston, built in 1907.

● Southern Pacific Railroad Station at 1174 East Commerce, built in 1902.

● Majestic Theater, 214 East Houston Street.

● Menger Soap Works, 400 North Laredo, built in 1850.

● Old First National Bank, 239 West Commerce, built in 1886.

● Schroeder-Yturri House at 1040 East Commerce, built in 1868.

● Ursuline Academy, 300 Augusta, built between 1851 and 1882.

1

1) *James Charles Wilson spent some time in jail in Mexico for invading Mexico with the Mier expedition in 1842. He escaped the following year and later served in the Texas legislature. Wilson County was named after him. 2) Little is left except this marker on the western outskirts of Floresville to indicate where the town of Lodi was. But Lodi and Sutherland Springs took turns serving as the county seat of Wilson County until 1871.*

WILSON COUNTY

Wilson County was organized in 1860, and it includes areas that had been part of Bexar and Karnes counties before that. There is a little oil and gas in Wilson County, but ranching and farming are the chief sources of income here.

The first settlers here were Mexican and Spanish families. But planters from the old South and German and Polish immigrants began moving in by the middle of the nineteenth century.

Wilson County was named for James Charles Wilson. He came to Texas from England in 1837. He missed the revolution, but he went to Mexico with the Mier Expedition in 1842. That was an unauthorized foray. Wilson and most of his companions were captured and imprisoned. Wilson escaped in 1843 and returned to Texas to serve in the legislature after Texas joined the United States.

The original county seat here was Sutherland Springs. The government moved back and forth between Sutherland Springs and Lodi a couple of times before it settled in Floresville in 1871. The moves apparently resulted from

1

2

1) *Only Georgia grows more peanuts than Texas. Peanuts grow in 117 of the 254 counties in Texas. This little monument on the grounds of the courthouse at Floresville signifies that peanuts are a major item in the economy of Wilson County. 2) The county jail at Floresville is older than the courthouse. The jail was completed in 1877. 3) Former Governor John Connally raises Santa Gertrudis cattle at his Picosa Ranch, outside Floresville. The breed was developed by the King Ranch. Prize animals like this one bring small fortunes at the periodic Santa Gertrudis auctions.*

3

squabbles among carpetbag officials. Sutherland Springs was a flourishing resort with some hot springs. Lodi was the oldest settlement in the county. But Floresville was on the route the San Antonio & Aransas Pass Railway company had picked for its tracks through Wilson County. It was named the county seat by popular election. The town site was donated by Josepha Flores de Barker, and it was named Floresville for her.

The present courthouse was completed in 1885. It was designed by Alfred Giles, and it was originally surrounded by a whitewashed wood fence. James Gordon designed the Wilson county jail that was completed in 1877. Both buildings were built of brick, but both were plastered over during a

1) Barbed wire came to Texas in 1879. The wire made it possible for landowners to fence in their property and fence other peoples' animals out. 2) The marker calls it a mission, but actually the Rancho de las Cabras was an outpost of the Mission San Francisco de la Espada in San Antonio, concerned mostly with raising cattle. 3) One of the oldest Masonic lodges in Texas holds its meetings in a stone building on the outskirts of La Vernia in Wilson County. The lodge building was built in 1854.

1

2

3

remodeling job the Works Progress Administration did in 1936.

Former Governor John Connally has a ranch outside Floresville where he raises Santa Gertrudis cattle.

One of the early ranchers here was Juan José María Erasmo de Jesús Seguin. He built a ranch near where Floresville is today, and he was one of the first landowners to experiment with growing cotton in Texas. Seguin was born a Spanish subject in San Antonio in 1782. He was a political and civic leader under the Spanish rule. He remained an influential citizen after Mexico won independence from Spain and he befriended the early Anglo colonists in Texas. Seguin sympathized with the Texans when they began fighting for independence and supplied horses and cattle to the Texas army.

Erasmo Seguin was hailed as a faithful friend of Texas when he died in 1857 here at his ranch in Wilson County. The city of Seguin in Guadalupe County was named for Seguin's son Juan Nepomucena Seguin, but Texans had more reservations about Juan than they had about his father.

Robert E. Lee stopped here in 1861 when he was a colonel in the U.S. Army. Texas had seceded from the Union and Lee was leaving the state. Lee was leaving because his native state of Virginia had not yet seceded from the Union. He stopped here because he was an old friend of the owner. The J. H. Polley house is still in excellent condition and the present owners open it to visitors occasionally.

Wilson County was in the middle of the fence wars in 1883 and 1884. The early cattlemen had been accustomed to grazing their cattle wherever there was anything for them to eat. No one worried about the ownership of the land. Most of it was not claimed by anybody. But landowners in Wilson County and other counties began fencing their land in 1883. The old time cattlemen had their cowhands cut the fences at night. They were repaired the next day, and cut again the next night. It went on like that until 1884 when the legislature passed a law requiring fence builders to put in gates every three miles. The same law made it a criminal offense to cut a fence. The ranchers and the fence builders gradually learned to live with each other.

There is a Peanut Festival in Floresville each year in October.

The site of the old Rancho de las Cabras outside Floresville is listed in the *National Register of Historic Places*. The ranch was an outpost of the Mission San Francisco de la Espada in San Antonio in the eighteenth century. Only ruins, foundations and partial walls remain. The State Department of Parks and Wildlife is acquiring the site and plans to turn it into an archaeological park.

Some other historical markers in Wilson County:

● La Vernia, the old Brahan Masonic Lodge on Blue Bonnet Drive, built in 1854 and still in use.

● La Vernia, the old Flores ranch house, off U.S. 181,

1) This once was the courthouse for Karnes County. A Pennsylvania Dutchman named Thomas Ruckman and a doctor named Lewis Owings established a trading post on the old wagon trail here. Their venture grew into a town they named Helena for the doctor's wife. The town became the county seat when Karnes County was established in 1854. This courthouse was built in 1873. But the railroad went the other way. The county seat moved to Karnes City. 2) The present Karnes County Courthouse in Karnes City was built in 1894.

three miles south of Calaveras, a big white adobe house built to withstand Indian attacks.

● Sutherland Springs, J. H. Polley house, on the Cibolo Creek.

KARNES COUNTY

Karnes County was established in 1854 from parts of what had been Bexar, Goliad and San Patricio counties. The county was named for Henry Wax Karnes. He was a captain in the Texas army during the revolution and an Indian fighter later. He died in 1840 before the county named for him was created.

The original county seat was Helena at the intersection of the present State Highway 80 and Farm Road 81. Helena was founded in 1852. It was on one of the wagon roads between Indianola and San Antonio, and it prospered for a time. But the town got a reputation as a hangout for bandits and rustlers, and the county's first railroad missed it. So Helena went into a decline and the county seat was moved to Karnes City in 1894. Helena is the next thing to a ghost town today. One story is that the richest rancher in the area made it worth the railroad's while to lay its tracks to miss Helena because he had vowed to do away with the town after his son was killed

1) Uranium is produced from a large open pit mine at Falls City in the northwest corner of Karnes County. Conoco is the operator of this mine. Chevron has a similar operation near Panna Maria. 2) No one anywhere was better pleased than the people of Panna Maria when a Polish cardinal was elevated to the papacy. Panna Maria claims to be the oldest Polish settlement in North America. A party of devout Polish Catholics, organized by Father Leopold Moczygemba, settled here in 1854. Their first church building was destroyed by lightning in 1877. They built the present Church of the Immaculate Conception the following year.

2

by outlaws here. The old courthouse at Helena is now a museum.

One of the surviving homes in old Helena is a big place John Ruckman built in 1857. Ruckman came here from Pennsylvania as did his brother, Thomas. Thomas Ruckman was one of the founders of Helena. He was the first postmaster, and he was also a merchant and banker. The home his brother John built is now the property of the Karnes County Historical Society.

Karnes City has not reached the status of a metropolis. The population is around three thousand. The people are mostly of Polish and Swedish extraction. The present courthouse was built in 1894. The town of Kenedy a few miles south of Karnes City is a little larger than the county seat.

There is substantial oil and gas production in Karnes County, and there is a uranium plant at Falls City on U.S. 181 at the northwestern edge of the county. Falls City takes its

1) At some time in the past, this building was a barn. Now it is the Panna Maria Post Office. Felix Snoga is the postmaster here. He is also the grocer and gas station operator. Some of the Polish settlers from Panna Maria moved a few miles north and established another community they named Cestohowa. 2) The Church of the Nativity of the Blessed Virgin Mary they built here is more imposing than the earlier church at Panna Maria. 3) A little of the history of the Polish settlements is preserved in a small museum at Runge. It is open usually, though, only on weekends.

2

3

name from a waterfall on the San Antonio River.

But the most picturesque place in Karnes County is probably Panna Maria on Farm Road 81 just east of State Highway 123. Panna Maria was founded by Polish Catholics in 1854, and it is said to be the oldest Polish settlement in Texas. The Church of the Immaculate Conception here is the oldest Polish Catholic church in North America. The original settlers here came from Poland by ship and then traveled overland from Galveston. Their first shelters were dugouts covered with brush. But they found plenty of stone in the area and eventually built themselves houses similar to those they knew in Poland. The devout settlers at Panna Maria were a novelty on the frontier, and they were harassed by cowboys and hoodlums until they persuaded the U.S. Army to send a cavalry detachment from San Antonio to keep order.

Panna Maria has been declining for a number of years. There is no real need for a town where it is. The people who live here now are still mostly Polish. They do their shopping and a good bit of their visiting at Felix Snoga's combination

Green C. DeWitt was one of the first U.S. citizens to get interested in colonizing Texas. He went to Mexico in 1822 and obtained permission in 1825 to settle colonists in the area that later became DeWitt and Gonzales counties. DeWitt chartered a schooner to carry colonists from the United States to Lavaca.

store, filling station and post office on Main Street. It is the only store in town.

Some of the early history of Karnes county is preserved in the little museum at the Polish settlement of Runge, a few miles southeast of Panna Maria on Farm Road 81. The museum is in an old store building on Main Street. It is open only on Saturday and Sunday afternoons, and there is no admission fee, but donations are welcome.

DEWITT COUNTY

DeWitt County was organized in 1846 from parts of what had been Gonzales, Goliad and Victoria counties. The county was named for a native of Kentucky. Green C. DeWitt obtained an empresario land grant from the government of Mexico in 1825. He was authorized to settle four hundred families along the Guadalupe, San Marcos and Lavaca rivers, and he moved his own family to the little settlement in this grant that became the city of Gonzales. Settlement of the area began very slowly. There were disputes between DeWitt and colonist Martin de Leon of Victoria, over boundaries. And there were Indian attacks. DeWitt died in 1835 before his settlement amounted to very much. Germans began settling in this area during the days of the republic, and Germans made up a majority of the population in DeWitt County by 1860.

The town of Cameron on the Guadalupe River was designated the county seat when DeWitt County was formed. The county government moved back and forth between

Part of the Guadalupe River in DeWitt County has been designated a National Historic Site because there are traces of Indian camps here dating back seven thousand years. Wagons and carts hauling freight from the Port of Indianola to San Antonio and beyond crossed the Guadalupe on a ferryboat Richard Chisholm operated here before bridges began to be built.

Cameron and Clinton a couple of times before it settled in Clinton in 1850. Clinton remained the county seat until 1876.

Clinton was on the west bank of the Guadalupe River where Richard Chisholm had a ferryboat crossing. Clinton and Cameron both were fairly prosperous towns when they were the county seat. Both declined when the county government moved away. This Cameron is not to be confused with the central Texas town of Cameron that is still the county seat of Milam County.

Indianola on Lavaca Bay was one of the chief ports on the Texas coast between the 1840s and 1870s. The wagons and ox-carts hauling freight from Indianola to San Antonio had to come through DeWitt County, and many of them crossed the Guadalupe on Richard Chisholm's ferryboat. This commerce and the legendary industriousness of the German settlers generated a prosperous economy for DeWitt County. There is some oil and gas in the county. But farming and ranching are bigger than oil and gas here. There are many turkey farms and Cuero calls itself the turkey capital of the world.

Cuero is the Spanish word for hide. The name originally was applied to a settlement a short distance from the present

1) People around Cuero have been raising turkeys for a long time. The town claims to be the turkey capital of the world. Some of the turkey raisers used to drive their birds along the streets to market in Cuero. Visitors exclaimed over the sight of the marching flocks of turkeys and that gave the people of Cuero an idea. 2) The idea grew into the Cuero Turkey Trot and Turkeyfest. Flocks of turkeys parade in the streets. There is a turkey race and entertainment and dancing in the streets. It is the only Turkeyfest we know of.

city. The name and the post office were moved to the present location because it was on the first rail line to reach DeWitt County. Many refugees from Indianola settled here after a hurricane wiped out Indianola in 1875. The county seat was moved to Cuero in 1876. The present courthouse was built in 1896. It is three stories tall, in what is called Romanesque Revival style. The courthouse is listed in the *National Register of Historic Places,* and so it is protected against nearly everything except fire, flood and lightning.

The DeWitt County Historical Museum at 312 E. Broadway in Cuero is open Thursday, Friday and Sunday afternoons. There is no charge. Exhibits emphasize local history and art. Texas artist E. M. "Buck" Schiwetz was born in Cuero in 1898, and he is still living in DeWitt County, on a ranch outside Westhoff. Schiwetz was educated as an architect, but he was more interested in sketching and painting. His sketches and paintings of Texas landscapes and old Texas buildings will forever remind future generations of what

1) *Texas artist Buck Schiwetz was trained to be an architect. This training shows in his sketches and paintings of Texas buildings and landmarks. One of his favorite subjects is Saint John's Evangelical Lutheran Church and graveyard at Meyersville, depicted here in a sketch Schiwetz did in 1957. 2) Many of the refugees from the hurricanes that destroyed Indianola in the 1870s came inland to this area and some of them decided to stay. A number of exhibits tracing the history of the area are on display in the DeWitt County Historical Museum.*

1) DeWitt County was organized in 1846, and the present DeWitt County Courthouse, built in 1896, is a national historic landmark. 2) Some of the refugees from Indianola helped to establish the St. Mark's Lutheran Church at 400 North Esplanade in Cuero. They were all Protestants, of course, but it is plain they had a good opinion of the architectural style the Catholic missionaries brought to this part of the world.

2

Texas was like in the early twentieth century when it was making the transition from frontier to urban culture.

A handsome church at 400 North Esplanade in Cuero looks like a Spanish mission. But it is German, not Spanish — Lutheran, not Catholic. St. Mark's Lutheran Church was built by some of the refugees from that hurricane at Indianola.

Robert Justus Kleberg was born outside Yorktown in

1) One of the most famous and most successful ranchers in the history of ranching was born in DeWitt County, near Yorktown. Robert Kleberg was the son of a German immigrant. He got into ranching by getting a law degree. He was hired to represent the King Ranch. He married Richard King's daughter Alice and he ran the King Ranch from the time Richard King died in 1885 until he died himself in 1932. 2) The old Eckhardt Mercantile Company building at West Main and Eckhardt in Yorktown is now a museum.

2

DeWitt County in 1853. His father was a German immigrant and chief justice of the county. Kleberg studied law and became the attorney for the King Ranch. He ran the ranch after Captain Richard King died, and he married King's daughter, Alice, in 1886. Kleberg County was named for Kleberg. There is a state marker at the site near Stubbs Station where Kleberg was born, but the house is no longer standing.

The Yorktown Historical Museum at West Main and

Houses built in this part of the world before air conditioning always had plenty of porches. They do more than provide a place for people to sit in the shade. They keep the heat of the sun from falling on the windows and walls of the living areas. Generous porches distinguish the old Cuero houses that bear historical markers, like the Emil Reiffert house at 304 West Prairie.

Eckhardt streets in Yorktown is open Thursday, Friday and Sunday afternoons. There is no fee, but donations are welcome. The building is the old Eckhardt Mercantile Company Building. The Eckhardt Mercantile Co. was established by one of the founders of Yorktown, Charles Eckhardt. He had been a merchant in Indianola. He was carrying on trade with the German settlers inland at New Braunfels. The wagon road between the port of Indianola and New Braunfels was a meandering and primitive trail. Eckhardt and John York formed a partnership in 1847 to improve the trade route and make a profit from it. York owned a lot of land around the present site of Yorktown. They hired a surveyor to plot a new road from Indianola to New Braunfels to pass through York's land, and they founded a town and called it Yorktown. Captain York was killed in a skirmish with the Comanches the year after the town was founded. Charles Eckhardt died about four years later.

But the town and Eckhardt's relatives and descendants prospered. By 1856, Yorktown had a theater and several hundred residents. In the 1870s, Robert C. Eckhardt operated a grist mill here, using a big windmill like those in Holland. People came from all over the surrounding area to have their

1

2

1) This house at 606 Terrell is known as the Gohmert-Summers place. 2) The Edward Mugge house and the other houses on this page are private residences. They are not generally open to the public but some of them sometimes are open during the Turkeyfest. The Mugge house is at 218 North Terrell Street. It was built in 1870. 3) This is the William Frobese house at 305 East Newman.

3

1) Only a state marker stands today where once stood one of the biggest boarding schools in Texas. The Baptists established Concrete College at the town of Concrete in 1865 when the town seemed to be flourishing. But people started moving away after the railroad missed the town and the school closed in 1881. Concrete College was collecting twenty dollars a month from each student during its heyday and that price covered tuition and room and board. 2) The Tex Tan Western Leather Company at Yoakum on the eastern edge of DeWitt County began as a small tannery in 1919. It is now one of the biggest leather goods companies in the country.

2

grain ground here. The first blacksmith shop opened in 1852, and there is a blacksmith operating in Yorktown still. A saloon founded here in 1895 operated until recently as the Horn Palace, and featured a collection of petrified wood and animal horns.

The town of Concrete on the Guadalupe above Cuero was a flourishing community in the 1850s and 1860s. The Concrete College was the largest boarding school in the state at one time. It was a Baptist school, co-ed, but very strict. Concrete went into a decline when the railroad passed it by and the college closed in 1881. There is a marker on U.S. 183, ten miles north of Cuero.

Some of the buildings in Cuero with historical markers are:

● Emil Reiffert house, 304 W. Prairie.
● Gohmert-Summers house, 606 Terrell.
● William Frobese home, 305 E. Newman.

1) Mosaic mural on the Municipal Building at Gonzales recalls the episode that produced the opening shot in the Texas war for independence. The Mexicans in 1835 demanded the return of a cannon they had lent the settlers here at Gonzales. The settlers turned the cannon on the Mexicans and the war was on. 2) This monument honors the heroes of the fighting at Gonzales. This city is often called the Lexington of Texas.

GONZALES COUNTY

The opening shot in the war that made Texas independent was fired at Gonzales. The town of Gonzales was burned twice. There is plenty of history here.

The settlement that became the city of Gonzales was founded by Green C. DeWitt in 1825 right after the Mexican government granted him permission to settle four hundred families in the area. The town was named for Rafael Gonzales. He was the governor of the Mexican state of Coahuila and Texas at the time DeWitt was starting his colony.

Indians burned the little settlement shortly after it was established. And the Texas army burned it in 1836. The Texas soldiers figured if they did not burn it, the Mexicans would. There had been trouble before, but it is generally conceded that the first shot of the Texas Revolution was fired here at Gonzales from a Mexican cannon by Texans.

Mexican authorities had lent a cannon to the settlers at Gonzales in the early 1830s. It was supposed to be used to discourage Indian attacks. The Mexican authorities realized by 1835 that the Texans were getting ready to secede. So the commander of the Mexican garrison at San Antonio sent a squad of soldiers to Gonzales to get the cannon back. The people of Gonzales refused to hand it over. Instead they buried it. They made up a battle flag with the legend Come and Take It, and they sent out a call for other Texans to come to Gonzales and help.

1) Another memorial erected during the Centennial year is the Gonzales Museum building. 2) This imposing monument stands near the spot where the defenders of Gonzales fired that first shot from the cannon the Mexicans were trying to get back. The small Mexican force sent out from San Antonio to get the cannon was not prepared to make that much of an issue of the matter, so the Mexicans returned to San Antonio. The outcome encouraged the rebels to march on San Antonio and on into history. This site is on Spur 95, off State Highway 97, three miles southwest of Gonzales.

1

2

A larger Mexican force arrived before the Texas reinforcements did. The Gonzales defenders stalled the Mexicans with conversation until John H. Moore of LaGrange arrived with a party of volunteers. The Texans then dug up the cannon, put it on wheels and attacked the Mexicans. It was not much of a battle. One Mexican soldier was killed and the others went back to San Antonio. But this skirmish encouraged the Texans and started the chain of events that ended at San Jacinto on April 21, 1836.

Stephen F. Austin came to Gonzales to take command of the Texas volunteers. He marched them to San Antonio where Ben Milam and Francis Johnson commanded them in the siege that forced the Mexican soldiers to surrender. The Texans occupied the Alamo, and that provoked the Mexican president Santa Anna to march north to put a stop to the revolutionary foolishness.

Gonzales sent additional volunteers to San Antonio in March of 1836 to help William Travis try to beat back Santa Anna's attack.

The convention of 1836 adopted the Declaration of

The Texas rebels took over San Antonio in December of 1835 and they held it until March 1836. The little Texas garrison was besieged by a superior Mexican force led by President Santa Anna. Sam Houston was on his way to San Antonio to try to turn the Mexicans back when he received word here that the Mexicans had wiped out the small garrison at the Alamo. Houston camped here long enough to gather up the available volunteers and begin his retreat toward San Jacinto.

Independence at Washington-on-the-Brazos on March 2, and named Sam Houston commander of the Texas army. Houston was on his way to the Alamo when word reached him here at Gonzales that the battle of the Alamo was already lost. Houston decided to burn Gonzales, and he began the retreat eastward that frightened Texas settlers into what came to be known as the Runaway Scrape.

Gonzales was rebuilt after Sam Houston defeated and captured Santa Anna at San Jacinto. The town became the county seat of Gonzales County when the county was established by the first Congress of the Republic in 1836. The present courthouse was built in 1894.

The Texas Centennial Commission built a monument in 1936 to the heroes of the fighting at Gonzales. The monument is on the square, west of the courthouse. The Gonzales

1

2

3

1) The Eggleston House is furnished with authentic antiques and it is open to visitors by arrangement with the curator of the Gonzales Memorial Museum. 2) Officials of Gonzales County believed in 1878 that the population of their county was going to grow a lot more than it did. So the new jail they built that year was designed to hold up to 200 prisoners. It turned out to be bigger than necessary. There is a new jail here, now, but the old one has been preserved and it is open to visitors. 3) The scaffold in the old Gonzales County Jail is a replica. The original gallows was taken out of the building sometime in the 1950s. At least two or three men were hanged here in the old Gonzales County Jail.

Museum in the Memorial Building built the same year at St. Lawrence and St. Louis streets houses exhibits recalling the role Gonzales and its citizens have played in the history of the state.

There are dozens of historical markers in and around Gonzales. There is one at the end of St. John Street marking the site where Sam Houston was camped when he learned the Alamo had fallen. There is another marker on U.S. 90-A, ten miles east of town, marking another Sam Houston campsite. There is a marker in the 200 block of St. Louis Street at the site of the old peach orchard where the settlers had the Mexican cannon buried. There is one on Spur 95, off State Highway 97, three miles southwest of town where the first shot of the revolution was fired from that cannon, and there

1) The original Gonzales County Courthouse burned in 1893 and the cornerstone for this building was laid in 1895. The Gonzales courthouse is a recorded Texas and national landmark. 2) The Braches House apparently was built sometime in the later 1830s. It is a private residence. 3) Louis and Anna Kennard built this Victorian mansion in 1895. Kennard was in the lumber business and he used the finest materials including Tiffany leaded glass.

2
3

is a marker at the intersection of U.S. Highway 90-A and Farm Road 794 where the Confederate army had a fort during the Civil War. Some of the earthworks are still visible.

A log cabin built in 1840 is still standing in the 1300 block of St. Louis Street in Gonzales. This is the Eggleston House. It has been restored, and it is furnished with authentic antiques from the middle nineteenth century. Tours of the Eggleston House can be arranged with the curator of the Gonzales Memorial Museum. The museum is open afternoons, from one to five, Wednesday through Sunday. There is no admission charge, but they are glad to have donations.

Four of the buildings in Gonzales are listed in the *National Register of Historic Places.* One is the old county jail on St. Lawrence Street, now privately owned. The register also lists the Gonzales County Courthouse, the old Kennard house at

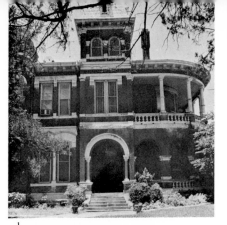

1) *James D. Houston built this mansion at 619 St. Lawrence Street in the 1890s with some of the money he made in the cattle business. The house has fifteen rooms and five bathrooms. It is known as the Lewis-Houston House. 2) Dr. John Curtis Jones built this home for his family in 1872. The mantels and many other interior details were carved by hand. 3) The Palmetto State Park on the San Marcos River north of Gonzales is a natural tropical garden. The area was called the Ottine Swamp before it was made a park in 1933.*

621 St. Louis Street, and the Braches house twelve miles southeast of town, off U.S. 90-A. The Braches house is a former stagecoach stop. It was built in the 1830s. It is private property.

There are state historical markers on a number of homes in Gonzales, including the Brown house at 834 Mitchell, the Chennault house at 324 St. Paul, the Reese home at 518 St. Francis, the Wells house at 829 Mitchell, and the Fauth house at 512 St. Peter Street. Some of the old homes are open during the Come and Take It celebrations in October. The weathervane on top of the fire house at 411 St. Lawrence was made originally for the home of cattleman R. A. Houston of

1) The Gonzales Warm Springs Foundation adjoining the Palmetto State Park provides treatment for victims of accidents and crippling diseases. 2) Miller's General Store at Waelder has been owned and operated by the same family for three generations. The barbecue they serve in the backroom here ranks with the best.

2

the T-41 Ranch. It is a longhorn steer, life-size.

The Palmetto State Park on the San Marcos River off U.S. 183 about ten miles north of Gonzales features an unusual botanical garden and provisions for swimming, fishing, picnicking and camping. This is one of the state's Class I parks. There is an admission fee.

The Gonzales Warm Springs Foundation adjoining the Palmetto State Park is built around a natural hot spring. It specializes in treatments for victims of accidents and crippling diseases.

Interstate Highway 10 cuts across the northern edge of Gonzales County, but there are no major cities on the freeway in this county. Just off I-10 on U.S. 90 is the old town of Waelder where the barbecue served in the backroom of

1) The man the city of Seguin is named for has been ranked as a Texas hero and as a traitor at different times. He contributed food and money to the Texas cause and he fought with the Texans at San Jacinto. But he moved to Mexico because of harassment. He was called a traitor when he took part in a raid into Texas in 1842. 2) The little building known as Los Nogales is older than the city of Seguin. When Juan Seguin was the postmaster this was the post office.

Miller's General Store has attracted national attention. Miller's Store has been run by the same family for three generations.

At the other end of the county, on U.S. Highway 87 near the Wilson County line, the little town of Nixon got some national attention during the years when Richard Nixon was holding and running for office. A national magazine published a picture during the Kennedy-Nixon campaign of a road sign near here that pointed left to Kenedy and right to Nixon. But the town of Nixon is not named for the president. It was named for rancher John T. Nixon.

GUADALUPE COUNTY

Guadalupe County was named for the Guadalupe River. The river was named by Captain Alonso de Leon in 1689 in honor of our Lady of Guadalupe. The county was created in 1846 from parts of Bexar and Gonzales counties.

The county seat is Seguin. This town was founded in 1838 by members of Matthew Caldwell's company of Texas Rangers. They originally called their town Walnut Springs. The name was changed in 1839 to honor Juan Nepomucena Seguin. Juan Seguin was one of the Mexican supporters of the Texas Revolution. He fought with the Texas army at San

The courthouses built in Texas in the 1930s have a certain resemblance to each other, a blandness that may have been a reaction to the overblown style the earlier courthouse builders favored. The appearance of this building announces that it is a government building built in the 30s. It is and it was. The Guadalupe County Courthouse at Seguin was built in 1936.

Jacinto, and he was later mayor of San Antonio. But some Texans suspected Seguin was really a Mexican sympathizer, and they made his life so uncomfortable he moved to Mexico in 1842. Seguin became an officer in the Mexican army. The way he explained it, President Santa Anna gave him a choice of going to jail or joining the army. Seguin returned to Texas in the fall of 1842 as a member of General Adrian Woll's invading force. Woll's Mexican army captured San Antonio and held it briefly. This was the maneuver that provoked the Texans into sending the Somervell and Mier expeditions into Mexico. Seguin managed to get permission to return to Texas later, but he never held a position of trust in Texas again. Juan Seguin died in Mexico and he was buried in Nuevo Laredo. The Mexicans returned his remains to Seguin in 1976 as a bicentennial gesture.

The first Anglo settler here was Humphrey Branch. He was a member of Green DeWitt's colony. The land where the city of Seguin is now was granted to Branch in 1830, and he settled on it in 1831. The city was designated the county seat a few days before the legislature actually established Guadalupe County in 1846. The city was incorporated in 1853. The present courthouse was built in 1936.

1) Colonel Joshua Young was a practical man. He built his house in Seguin with a roof that was also a water tank. The roof caught rainwater which also kept the house cool. 2) The Humphrey house in Seguin was originally built on another site. The house was sawed up and hauled here in sections by teams of oxen in the 1860s.

But it is plain that people were living where Seguin is long before the Branch family came. The evidence is a little brick house at River Street and Liveoak. This building is known as Los Nogales, also called the Juan Seguin Post Office. Los Nogales was built sometime before 1822. It may date back to the 1760s. The location is known to have been a stopping point on the old Spanish trail. The bricks the building is made of were made by hand and baked in the sun. It was a technique the Spanish used before they began using adobe.

The old building has been a home at various times, and it served as the post office when Juan Seguin was postmaster here. Los Nogales is listed in the *National Register of Historic Places.* Two other buildings in Seguin are listed in the register. One of them is the Zorn House, also known as Sebastapol, at West Court and North Erkel streets. Sebastapol was built by Colonel Joshua Young in the 1850s as a home for his sister. It is made of concrete with a flat roof designed to hold water. The house is now owned by the Seguin Conservation Society.

The other Seguin building listed in the *National Register of Historic Places* is the Humphrey house at 902 North Austin Street. Dr. Benjamin Humphrey moved this house here from the village of Prairie Lea shortly after the Civil War. He had it cut into three sections and the sections were hauled here by ox teams. The house was added onto several times after it was re-assembled here. It is privately owned.

1) The dashing Texas Ranger Captain Jack Hays was married in the old Magnolia Hotel. The Hayses then went to California. Jack became sheriff of San Francisco County and made a fortune as one of the promoters of the city of Oakland. 2) It is an apartment house today, but this was originally the Magnolia Hotel, built in 1842. 3) The people of Seguin are particularly proud of their oak trees. Some of the trees here are believed to be hundreds of years old and several of them have names. 4) They call this one the Hanging Oak. They don't cut down old oak trees very readily here.

The Magnolia Hotel at 203 South Crockett Street still looks on the outside very much the way it looked when it was new in 1842. The building has been restored and divided into apartments. One of the celebrities of the frontier days was married here. This is where Captain Jack Hays married Susan Calvert. Hays was one of the most famous early members of the Texas Rangers. He was the victor in fights with the Comanches at Enchanted Rock and Bandera Pass.

1) *The Friedens United Church of Christ at Geronimo is the Timmerman sisters' church and they personally decorate it for Easter and Thanksgiving every year. Watergate prosecutor Leon Jaworski spent part of his boyhood here at Geronimo. His father was once pastor of the Friedens Church. 2) The Timmerman sisters of Geronimo have been doing good deeds for the community, their church and for the Seguin High School football teams for many years. The Timmerman sisters all live together in the house their late father built in 1892.*

2

St. Andrews Episcopal Church at Nolte and Crockett has had a new rock exterior added since it was built in 1876. The stained glass and the wood carving are original.

The Andrew Neil Church House had a loft where slaves could attend services when it was built by the Baptists in 1854.

The First Methodist Church was built at Washington and Camp streets in 1849. The building later became the home of the Nolte National Bank.

The Max Starcke Park on the Guadalupe at Seguin is an unusually fine municipal park. Some of the oak trees here are believed to be more than five hundred years old.

This county has always been noted for its livestock, and the horse Teddy Roosevelt rode up San Juan Hill in Cuba during

1) Some old railroad passenger depots have been turned into museums. The old depot at Seguin is being used now by a truck line. 2) Benton Donegan has restored the old rock cabin where his great grandfather once was stationed as a Texas Ranger. Ben and Henry McCullough called this place Hardscramble when they built it with local stone in 1841. Donegan's great grandfather Nathaniel Benton occupied the outpost for a time after the McCulloughs moved on in 1858. Donegan acquired it and put it back together. Hardscramble is not accessible to the public. It is about eight miles east of Seguin.

the Spanish-American War came from here. The horse was given to Roosevelt by a cousin. It was named Texas, of course.

The Guadalupe River furnished power for many mills during the pioneer days, and hydroelectric power plants were developed about as early here as anywhere in the state. The little lake created by the hydroelectric plant at McQueeney became one of the early centers of water skiing.

McQueeney is about four miles upstream from Seguin. A few miles farther north at Geronimo, seven sisters named Timmerman share a house their German father built in 1892 on Timmerman Lane. They are pillars of the Friedens church and the biggest fans of the Seguin High School football team. The Timmermans decorate the Friedens church for Thanksgiving and Easter, and they entertain the football team at dinner every season.

Watergate prosecutor Leon Jaworski began his education in a one-room schoolhouse at Geronimo. His father was pastor, at the time, of the church now known as the Friedens United Church of Christ at Geronimo.

A German nobleman established the first settlement in Comal County. Prince Carl of Solms-Braunfels called his settlement New Braunfels. 1) The prince did not stay here long. He had a lot to go back to. He was related to the King of Prussia and he lived in this castle at Braunfels on the Lahn. He hardly needed a new place to live. 2) The prince was a member of a syndicate some German blue bloods formed to sponsor settlements in Texas.

2

COMAL COUNTY

The successful revolution of the residents of Texas against the government of Mexico captured the imagination of people all over the world. And people were attracted to the new republic from many places. A group of noblemen in Germany formed an organization they called the Adelsverein in 1842 for the purpose of sponsoring German settlements in Texas. The society was dissolved five years later. But it had a hand in settling more than seven thousand Germans in Texas during the years it operated. Prince Carl of Solms-Braunfels was one of the members of the Adelsverein. He came to Texas in 1844 and scouted around looking at several areas before he bought some land on the Comal River and started the settlement that became New Braunfels. The prince went back to Germany a few months later. But the Germans he had brought here with him put down roots and built a prosperous community.

Texas was annexed to the United States a few months after New Braunfels was established. The Texas legislature created Comal County from parts of Bexar, Gonzales and Travis counties in 1846, and New Braunfels was designated the county seat. The present courthouse was built in 1898.

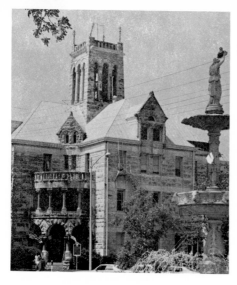

1

2

3

1) New Braunfels became the county seat when Comal County was organized in 1846. The present county courthouse was built in 1898. 2) The Comal river rises from a spring in northwest New Braunfels and it empties into the Guadalupe River just four miles from this point. The Comal is the only river in the United States that begins and ends in the same city. 3) Major railroads ran excursion trains to Landa Park in New Braunfels once. The last excursion train left a great many years ago, but there is a little tourist train operating here now. 4) Riding rafts and inner tubes through the rapids on the Comal has been a popular sport for many years.

4

Rudolph Nauerdorf built a hotel he called the Guadalupe on Main Plaza in New Braunfels in the early 1850s. The hotel became the Schmitz Hotel and the new owners added a third floor. Later it was renamed the Plaza. It was a fairly fancy place for a frontier town. The old hotel is still in business, or it will be when the New Braunfels Conservation Society finishes restoring it.

Comal county was named for the Comal River. This may be the shortest real river in the United States. The Comal begins in a cluster of springs in the northwest section of the present city of New Braunfels. The distance it travels from here until it spills into the Guadalupe River is only about four miles. The river is entirely within the city limits of New Braunfels. But it is a picturesque stream, clear and cold. The Comal is the central attraction in Landa Park. The upper reaches of the little river were bought by J. M. Merriweather in the 1850s. He developed a gristmill and a sawmill to utilize the water power. A German immigrant named Joseph Landa bought Merriweather out in 1859. Landa added an ice plant and an electric plant to the industrial complex on the little river. An observant early traveler named N. A. Taylor wrote in 1877 that Texas would become one of the principal centers of population in the United States. He predicted that the leading cities would be Houston, Galveston and New Braunfels. It was the age of water power, and Taylor was impressed by the potential of the swift streams around New Braunfels. The water is still flowing just as swiftly, but other forms of power took over before New Braunfels achieved the prominence Taylor predicted.

The beauty of the Comal River impressed the daughter of

1) *The Prince Solms has modern air conditioning and all the conveniences. It is a restoration and then some. The present owners have imported some fittings and fixtures and architectural refinements somewhat fancier than the original. 2) The Prince Solms was only a couple of years old when this picture was made in 1901. It was the Comal Hotel then, sturdy but plain. It has been an operating hotel almost continuously since it was built in 1898 and 1899. 3) Expensive antiques fill the guest rooms and public rooms of the Prince Solms Inn today.*

railroad magnate Jay Gould. Helen Gould announced that she thought there should be a park here. Her daddy's I.G.N. railroad and the Missouri, Kansas & Texas Railroad both thought well of her suggestion, and the area around the headwaters of the Comal was turned into a park in 1898. Both the I.G.N. and the M.K.T. ran tourist excursions here. Landa park is now owned by the city of New Braunfels. And there is

The Lindheimer House in New Braunfels is listed in the National Register of Historic Places. It is an example of German fachwerk construction. The framework is of heavy squared timbers, the spaces between the timbers are filled in with stone and brick and the surface is plastered over. This house was built about 1852. Ferdinand Lindheimer was a pioneer botanist and journalist. He was a guide for Prince Carl so he probably had a good bit to do with the selection of the site for New Braunfels.

still a railroad. It is a miniature tourist train operated by Mr. and Mrs. Bill McCrary. The little train carries visitors on a trip around the park that takes about ten minutes. It operates every day of the year, rain or shine.

One of the popular tourist pastimes here is shooting the rapids on the Comal on floats or in old inner tubes at Camp Warneke or Prince Solms Park.

The food specialties in New Braunfels are German sausage and German pastry. There is a sausage festival every year in November. It is called the Wurstfest and it lasts for ten days, beginning around November 1. The quantities of sausage and beer consumed each year are phenomenal.

Four of the buildings in New Braunfels are listed in the *National Register of Historic Places.* They are the old Plaza Hotel on the Main Plaza, built in 1851, said to have been the first hotel in Texas to have running water piped in, the Stephen Klein house built in 1846 at 131 South Seguin Street, the Lindheimer House built in 1852 at 489 Comal Street, open daily except Monday in the summer, and on Saturday and Sunday afternoons the rest of the year, and the first protestant church built in 1875 at 296 South Seguin Street.

57

1

1) The Faust is not as old as the Plaza and the Prince Solms. This hotel was built in 1928. It has been carefully restored and many of the original fixtures and furnishings have been retained. 2) Some of the history of the early days in New Braunfels is illustrated in displays here in the Sophienburg Memorial Museum. 3) Visitors to New Braunfels will find several places ready and willing to satisfy any inclination they may have to sample the sausages, pastries and beer the Germans are noted for. This is so the year around and at least doubly so during the annual Wurstfest in the fall.

2

3

1

2

3

1) *Some people say this is the oldest Lutheran church in Texas. This is St. Martin's Evangelical Lutheran Church of Hortontown. It was built about 1850. 2) The little town of Gruene has been discovered by artists and conservationists fairly recently. The first settlers came around 1850, but H. D. Gruene gave the settlement its name when he established a general store here in 1878. His gingerbread home has recently been restored. 3) An authentic old gristmill in Gruene has been turned into a restaurant and its owners have left the rough exterior of the building just like they found it.*

There are state historical markers on a number of other buildings here. Some of these are the Dietz Cottage at 197 East Mill Street, the Breustedt Kitchen on State Highway 46 South, the Groos house at 228 South Seguin, the Koester home at 421 South Seguin, the Moeller house at 212 West Austin, the Bevenroth house at 251 South Seguin, and the Scholl house at 550 Comal Street.

The Phoenix Saloon once stood at 1932 West San Antonio

1) The dancehall in Gruene is said to be the oldest surviving dancehall in the state. The story here is that Mr. Gruene built it because it annoyed him to see the young people of his town going off to spend their money in New Braunfels on Saturday nights. Gruene is pronounced green. 2) The Guadalupe River is the favorite stream of many Texas canoe and rafting enthusiasts. This is the river below the Canyon Lake dam. Fly fishermen are also partial to this stretch of water.

2

Street in New Braunfels where the Jacob Schmidt Company is today. Willie Gebhardt ran the restaurant in the Phoenix Saloon, and it is said that he served his first chili here. Gebhardt started making chili powder commercially in New Braunfels in 1896, and he produced his first canned chili con carne here in 1908. The company Gebhardt founded is headquartered today in San Antonio, still making chili and chili powder.

The Sophienburg Museum at 401 West Coll Street in New Braunfels preserves some of the history of the early German settlement. The museum is on the site where Prince Carl Solms-Braunfels built the log fortress that served as administrative headquarters for his colony. The museum is open from ten to five Mondays through Saturdays and from one to five on Sundays.

Two of the early hotels in New Braunfels have recently

1

1) Canyon Lake on the Guadalupe above New Braunfels is more than a resort. Increasing numbers of people are building permanent homes in the hills here because the area is reasonably close to both San Antonio and Austin. 2) The general store at Fischer is almost all there is to Fischer. This is also the gas station and the Post Office. It has been operated by members of the Fischer family since it was established. Fischer is on Ranch Road 32 in northern Comal County.

2

been restored and put back in operation. They are the Prince Solms Inn, 295 E. San Antonio Street near the Comal River, and the Faust Hotel at 240 S. Seguin.

The Natural Bridge Limestone Caverns are about seventeen miles west of New Braunfels off Farm Road 1863. The caverns are open every day. There is an admission fee.

The little village of Gruene just north of New Braunfels was settled in the 1850s, and there are several nineteenth century German homes and commercial buildings here. Gruene has recently been added to the *National Register of Historic Places.*

The Guadalupe is one of the most scenic rivers in Texas. The drive up the river from New Braunfels to Sattler along the river, and the drive along Ranch Road 32 above Canyon Lake are among the more scenic routes in the New Braunfels area. But there are many others. Pick up some German

This is the new part of the Kendall County Courthouse at Boerne. An older section, behind this, was built in 1870. The older section is the original Kendall County Courthouse.

sausage and pastry in New Braunfels and have a picnic on the way.

If you keep a sharp watch while you are traveling along Ranch Road 32, you may spot the settlement of Fischer. Herman Fischer settled here in 1853, and there have been Fischers here ever since. But there have never been very many other people, and Fischer is still a very small settlement. The center of the community is the Fischer General Store and Post Office. The postmaster here always has been a member of the Fischer family, and the old store where the post office is still looks much as it did in the nineteenth century. Tourists often try to buy the fixtures and the signs, but the Fischers say they are not interested in selling.

The Corps of Engineers maintains seven parks around Canyon Lake. All of them have public launching ramps, and most of them have provisions for camping. Farm Road 306 gives access to the parks on the east and north shore; FM 2673 serves the south and west shores.

Fly fishermen are partial to the waters of the Guadalupe below the Canyon Dam. They have been stocked with rainbow and brown trout.

KENDALL COUNTY

Kendall County has a monument to Union sympathizers, and it once had a communist commune. The county was formed from parts of Comal, Bexar and Blanco counties during the Civil War. It was named for George W. Kendall. He was a pioneer sheep and goat rancher and one of the founders of the *New Orleans Picayune* newspaper. Boerne has been the county seat from the outset. It is pronounced *bernie*. The

1

1) Kendall County was named for an adventuresome newspaperman. George W. Kendall was one of the founders of the New Orleans Picayune. He liked to get out and cover the news himself. He went with the Texans on their ill-advised expedition to Santa Fe in 1841 and he went to Mexico with the American troops in 1846 as a correspondent. He raised sheep and goats here and traveled to New Orleans periodically to take care of his newspaper interests. 2) Ye Kendall Inn on Main Plaza in Boerne began catering to travelers in 1859. It is now a private home.

2

town was established about 1851 and named for a refugee German poet. A small band of German intellectuals had founded what they called the Communistic Colony of Bettina on the Llano River some distance north of here about four years earlier. Their idea was to share the work and share the proceeds, but they had more education than they had practical skills and the colony failed after a year or two. A few of the more determined colonists then founded a commune they called Tusculum here in what is now Kendall County. Tusculum was about two miles west of Boerne. Tusculum failed, too, about the time Boerne was established. At least one of the commune founders stayed on and lived out his life in Texas. He was Dr. Ferdinand Herff. He became a very

1) The Theis House at 104 West Newton Street in Boerne is a pioneer museum. The house was built in the late 1850s and the exhibits include some early Texas furnishings and tools. The museum does not have regular hours. But it usually is open on Charter Day in October. 2) The Historical House Museum on Blanco Street in Boerne is also known as the King House. It is maintained by the Boerne Area Historical and Preservation Society.

2

distinguished surgeon and civic leader before he died in San Antonio in 1908.

The courthouse in Boerne is one of the oldest in the state. The back part of it was built in 1870 and the front part was added in 1901.

Ye Kendall Inn on U.S.-87 in downtown Boerne was a stagecoach stop in the 1850s. It is now a private residence.

There are two small museums in Boerne. The Theis House at 104 W. Newton Street is open by appointment and during the Boerne Area Historical Preservation Society's Charter Day Celebration in October. The museum features pioneer furnishings and tools. The house itself was built in the late 1850s. The King House on Blanco Street is also open only by appointment except during the Charter Day Celebration. There is no admission fee at either of these places.

There are two limestone caves open to visitors in Kendall County. The Cascade Caverns are off I-10 about five miles southeast of Boerne. The caverns are open all day every day, and there are tours every thirty minutes. The tour takes about

Underground rivers and streams have carved spectacular caverns in the limestone formations under this part of the state. This is a waterfall in Cascade Cavern outside Boerne. There are conducted tours here every half hour, all day, every day. The Cave Without a Name in the same area is also open to visitors every day. There is an admission fee at both caves.

1) The German settlers in this part of the Texas hill country had mostly been here only a few years when Texas decided to secede from the Union. Many of the German settlers were opposed to secession. This memorial stands in Comfort in memory of a party of Union sympathizers ambushed by Confederates as they tried to make their way out of Texas to Mexico in 1862. 2) A little stone house Frederick Meyer built in downtown Comfort in 1869 has recently been restored by Ann McGrath. The adjoining Meyer Hotel has also been restored and it is accommodating guests again. Ms. McGrath calls the place the Gast Haus. The address is 952 High Street.

2

one hour. There are campsites and trailer connections at the Cascade Caverns. There is an admission fee here and also at the Cave Without a Name, off Ranch Road 474, eleven miles northeast of Boerne. This cave, also, is open every day.

The only monument erected in Texas to honor people loyal to the Union during the Civil War is in Comfort at the western edge of Kendall County. Many of the German settlers in the hill country here opposed secession from the United States in 1861. They were not very popular with the Confederate sympathizers. A party of sixty-five Union sympathizers headed for Mexico in the summer of 1862, apparently intending to go on from there to the northern United

1) Theodore Goldbeck built a small log house and a small store at Main Street and Seventh, in Comfort, in 1854. August Faltin bought the property in 1856. He did well and he expanded the house with a fachwerk addition in 1858. The house is still in sound condition and still in the Faltin family. 2) August Faltin replaced the original Goldbeck store building in 1879 with this building designed by architect Alfred Giles. This building, too, is still in the Faltin family.

States. The Union sympathizers were ambushed by ninety-four southern cavalrymen. Nineteen of the Union sympathizers were killed in the battle, and nine others were wounded and later executed. The battle was fought near Fort Clark, some distance south of here. But most of the men killed were from this area. And their friends and relatives put up a monument to them. It still stands on High Street in Comfort.

Other recorded historic sites in Comfort include the Faltin house on Seventh Street near Altgelt Square and the Rice house on State Highway 27 at Cypress Creek.

An old stagecoach inn and lodging house built in 1869 by Frederick Meyer has been restored and put back in the business of renting rooms. Ann McGrath restored the old

Some of the stone buildings still standing around the community of Sisterdale go back to the 1840s and 1850s. Sisterdale is in central Kendall County, on Sister Creek, just north of the Guadalupe. An early traveler said the place reminded him of a nest of robbers in the Alps, it was so serene and secure.

place in the early 1970s. She calls it the Gast Haus. It is located in downtown Comfort.

Some German intellectuals established a settlement in the valley of Sister Creek in the 1840s. It was said they had the best school in Texas. Their settlement was not a big success economically. It was soundly built, though. Some of the original buildings are still here, and the valley is listed in the *National Register of Historic Places.* But the property is all privately owned and not open to the public. Sisterdale is just north of the Guadalupe River where Farm Road 473 and Farm Road 1376 meet, near the center of Kendall County.

N. A. Taylor visited here in 1877. He wrote in his journal, *Two Thousand Miles in Texas on Horseback,* that Sisterdale reminded him of a nest of robbers in the Alps except that everybody living here was so happy and contented.

BANDERA COUNTY

Bandera County is the center of the dude ranching business in Texas. There is not much other industry here. The county has little oil or gas production. The income from farming and ranching is not great. Accommodating tourists is the principal business here.

Bandera County was organized in 1856, from parts of Bexar and Uvalde counties. The town of Bandera is the county seat. The present courthouse was built in 1891. Bandera County and the town of Bandera were named for the Bandera Mountains in the northwestern corner of the county. The mountains also figure in most of the early history of the

It is not easy to say where the Bandera Mountains got their name. There are two stories and in both, the Apaches were living here and making raids on the Spanish settlement at San Antonio. In both stories, Spanish troops marched up here, did battle with the Apaches and won. In one version, the fight ended with an agreement that the Indians would stay north of the mountain pass here and a flag (bandera, in Spanish) was hoisted in the pass to make it plain where the line was. In the other version, the mountains were named Bandera because that was the name of the commander of the Spanish troops.

area. It is not altogether clear how the mountains got their name.

According to the *Handbook of Texas,* a Spanish general named Bandera was sent out about 1720 to put a stop to Apache raids on the settlement at San Antonio. The story is that the general and his troops trailed the Apaches into these mountains and the Apaches tried to ambush them in a pass here. The ambush attempt failed and the Spaniards scattered the Apaches. According to this story, the victorious general's name was applied to the mountains and to the pass where the fight occurred.

Anyway, the pass already was named Bandera Pass when a party of Texas Rangers commanded by Captain Jack Hays and a band of Comanches clashed here in 1842. That battle was a draw. The Comanches ambushed the rangers and the Comanche chief and six rangers were killed in the fighting in the pass. Both sides pulled back at nightfall, and by the following morning, the Indians had buried their dead and disappeared. Bigfoot Wallace was one of the rangers in Hays'

Ranchers in Bandera County raise lots more goats than cows, but Bandera says it is the cowboy capital of the world. There are some real cowboys here, but most of them are just sometime and parttime cowboys. They are the dudes. Bandera is the center of the dude ranching business in Texas.

company in that fight.

The first settlers did not move in here until about ten years after the battle between the rangers and the Comanches. A few people came in about 1852 to build a sawmill to make shingles out of the cypress trees growing along the Medina River. Several Polish families came in 1855 to work in the sawmill, and the town of Bandera grew out of this settlement. There was a wagon road between here and San Antonio and the round trip took about seven days. A party of Mormons led by Elder Lyman Wight moved into the area in 1854. These Mormons were at odds with Brigham Young and his idea of establishing a headquarters for the Mormon church in the rocky mountain area. They had come to Texas about 1845. And they had established settlements and mills on two or three other streams before they came here. Their previous settlements had been wiped out by floods. Wight and the Mormons established a sawmill on the Medina, opposite Bandera, and they moved downstream a little later and established the community of Mountain Valley. But they did not prosper, and Wight was thinking of returning to the North when he died in 1858. Wight was buried in the Mormon cemetery at Zodiac, near Fredericksburg, and many of his followers moved to the Mormon colony in Shelby County, Iowa.

The Frontier Times Museum at 506 Thirteenth Street in Bandera has a collection of pioneer tools and implements and

1) *One of the buildings in Bandera old enough to qualify as a registered state landmark is on Main Street at Cypress. The old Huffmeyer Store building now houses the Pollock Pharmacy and the Trading Post Western Wear store.* 2) *Residents of buildings bearing state historical markers often find strangers on their premises, looking for the history. The markers do not mean the buildings are public or open to the public. The Jureczki house is a private residence.* 3) *The two oldest Polish Catholic churches in the United States are in Texas. The oldest is in Panna Maria in Karnes County. The second oldest is here in Bandera. This is Saint Stanislaus Church.*

western paintings. There is a small admission fee. This museum is often closed.

Sites with state historical markers here include:

- Bandera's First Bank, at 11th and Cypress.
- Bandera Methodist Church, Hackberry and 11th streets.
- Bandera Jail, on the courthouse square.
- The Jureczki house, 7th and Cypress streets.
- The old Huffmeyer Store at Cypress and Main.
- The St. Stanislaus Catholic Church at 703 Cypress.

There is also a state marker at Bandera Pass, ten miles north of the city of Bandera on Farm Road 689.

Historian Jack Maguire claims that the U.S. Navy rented a bat cave here in Bandera County during World War II. Maguire says the navy recruited a squadron of Mexican free-tailed bats and outfitted them with tiny incendiary bombs and then dropped them over Tokyo. The idea was that the incendiary bombs would ignite as the bats roosted around the Japanese capital. There never were any fires credited to the bats from Bandera County, but it makes a good story.

The maple trees in the Sabinal River Canyon here in

1) The Bandera County Courthouse was built in Bandera in 1891. The television antenna was added later. 2) The Frontier Times Museum has displays that include a collection of firearms, a collection of bells, various Indian relics and relics from the frontier days. The sign says it is open every day except Monday, but we have found it closed several times. 3) The old jail building on the square in Bandera looks like it might have been built as part of a western movie set. But it really was the Bandera County Jail in 1881 and for a good many years afterward. It is now a museum.

2   3

western Bandera County make a rare sight when the leaves turn red in the fall. The State Department of Parks and Wildlife has acquired twenty-eight hundred acres in the canyon, north of Vanderpool. The area opened to visitors for the first time in the summer of 1979. It is preserved in its natural state for hiking and primitive camping. The parks people plan sixty campsites among the maples and at least half of them will be reachable only on foot. The entrance to the Lost Maples State Natural Area is off Farm Road 187 about four miles north of Vanderpool.

There will be another natural park here a little later. Louise Merrick is donating nearly five thousand acres of land to the state for a hill country natural area. This land is along the southern boundary of Bandera County and part of it is in Medina County. It is about two miles southeast of Tarpley.

A Portuguese aristocrat gave the area that is Medina County much of its character when he brought several hundred settlers here from the Province of Alsace in the 1840s. Henri Castro had struck up a friendship with President Sam Houston and Houston gave him a grant of land in the Medina valley. Castroville is one of the towns the Castro colonists founded.

MEDINA COUNTY

The area that is Medina County today has seen a lot of coming and going over a long period of time. The old Spanish road from San Antonio to Laredo cut through the southeastern corner of this county, as Interstate 35 does today. And the old stage and wagon road from San Antonio to El Paso crossed this county from east to west, as U.S. Highway 90 still does.

This area was settled by Alsatians brought in by Henri Castro in the days of the Republic. Henri Castro was born in France but descended from a noble Portuguese family. He was working with a French banking house when the new Republic of Texas was negotiating foreign loans. He did the Republic some favors and President Sam Houston made Castro the Texas consul general in Paris. A little later Houston gave Castro a grant to settle European immigrants on some land west of San Antonio. Castro decided Alsatians were the people most likely to make a go of it.

Castro brought over several hundred Alsatians and he founded the towns of Castroville, D'Hanis, Quihi and Vandenburg. Castroville was established first, in 1844, in the month of September. The town was laid out around a square called September Square and the streets were named for European capitals and for friends of Henri Castro. The Alsatians built sturdy stone houses resembling those in the Rhineland they had come from. Many of those houses are still standing and the village of Castroville is listed in the *National Register of Historic Places*.

1) The old Landmark Inn at Castroville has been donated to the Texas Department of Parks and Wildlife. The Department is restoring the buildings and the inn should be open and offering accommodations to travelers again by the middle of 1980. It is a small place. There are just eight rooms. 2) The old building behind the Landmark Inn, on the banks of the Medina River, has been a gristmill and a primitive electric power plant at various times. It was built in the 1850s.

2

The Landmark Inn here is owned now by the State Parks and Wildlife Department and it is being restored to be operated by the department as an inn. This building was originally a home and store, all on one floor. It was built in 1849 by Cesar Monod. John Vance bought the place in 1854. He added the second floor and turned the building into an inn. Castroville was on the main road to El Paso, and it was about one day out of San Antonio, at the rate wagons and coaches traveled in those days. So business was brisk. The Castroville post office was in this building from 1867 to 1870. George Haass bought the property between the inn and the Medina River in the 1850s, and he developed a gristmill at the water's edge.

J. T. Lawler bought the entire property including the inn and Vance's home and the Haass mill in 1925. Lawler saw that the gristmill could be turned into a power plant to supply

1) Many of the sturdy stone buildings the original settlers built are still standing and still occupied in Castroville and D'Hanis. This is the Louis Haller house in Castroville. It was built in the 1870s. 2) The Catholic settlers of Castroville lost no time building a church. The first one they built in 1847 is still solid, but they outgrew it very shortly. It is on the grounds of the Moye Academy.

electricity to Castroville, and that is what he did. He also developed a water supply system later acquired by the city of Castroville.

The inn and the mill passed to Lawler's sister Ruth after Lawler died, and Ruth Lawler donated the property to the State Department of Parks and Wildlife in 1974. The department expects to have the inn refurbished and open for business by the middle of 1980.

The Tarde Hotel in Castroville was once regarded as one of the finest stopping places on the frontier. This building is now a private home. Robert E. Lee was a guest here when it was a hotel. Many other buildings put up by the original settlers in the days of the Republic are still standing here.

The first Catholic church was built in 1847. It is still standing on the grounds of what is now called the Moye High School. The church was outgrown shortly after it was finished. A larger church was built on Angelo Street in 1849, and a still larger one was built next door to that one in 1868. All three of these churches were named St. Louis, in honor of the French king. All three buildings are still standing. The first pastor of the first St. Louis Catholic Church here was Father Claude Dubuis. He went on from here to become bishop of Galveston. Dubuis and another priest personally built the first rectory across the street from the original church. The rectory has been changed and improved, but it is still standing. This and buildings like it all around Castroville give this town the atmosphere of a European village. Some of the old homes here are open during the Castroville Garden Club Pilgrimage each year in April.

1) The Castroville Catholics built their second church on Angelo Street in 1849, and then they built this larger church next door in 1868. 2) The Sisters of Divine Providence established a school here in 1868 and named it for the founder of their order, the Reverend John Moye. It is a retreat and convent, now. 3) The first pastor of the first St. Louis Catholic Church here was Father Claude Dubuis. He and another priest personally built the original rectory.

Medina County was established by the Texas state legislature in 1848, and Castroville was the original county seat. There was a stone courthouse. It is still standing and serving now as the Castroville City Hall. The people here are not given to throwing away or tearing down anything that is usable.

They are not much inclined to try anything new, either. At least they were not in 1880. The Galveston, Harrisburg & San Antonio Railroad was plotting its route westward from San Antonio that year. Castroville would have been a logical stopping point. But the railroad wanted a bonus of 100,000 dollars to lay its tracks through Castroville. The people of Castroville decided they could do without it. The railroad company detoured around Castroville with the usual result. A

Castroville was designated as the county seat when Medina County was first established, and the people here built a courthouse of native stone. The first railroad skipped Castroville. Hondo became the county seat, but the old Castroville courthouse is still doing duty. It is the Castroville City Hall, now.

new town developed on the rail line, west of Castroville. It was named Hondo, and in 1892 it became the county seat of Medina County because it was growing and prospering, and Castroville was not. The present courthouse in Hondo was built in 1893.

The influence of the railroads eventually waned, too. And the passenger depot built in Hondo in 1897 has been moved to another location and turned into a museum. The station is now the headquarters of the Medina County Museum. It is at Eighteenth Street and Avenue X. The displays trace the history of the county. The museum also has an old, one-room schoolhouse and some old carriages. It is open every day during the summer months and on Saturdays and Sundays the rest of the year. There is a small admission fee. The Hondo Chamber of Commerce has a good map of the Medina County area, pinpointing historic sites and suggesting sightseeing routes. The Chamber of Commerce is in the municipal building in Hondo.

Historic buildings in Hondo include the old Fohn-Bless Store at 1020 Eighteenth Street and the old Fred Metzger House at 1003 Sixteenth Street.

D'Hanis is another town founded by members of the original Castro colony in 1847. It is on U.S. 90, west of

1) A collection of carriages is one of the features of the Medina County Museum in Hondo. The museum overflows into a couple of other buildings, but it is centered around the old railroad passenger depot, at Eighteenth Street and Avenue X. 2) The Medina County Museum has an assortment of tools and utensils used by the early settlers and there is an old one-room school house on the grounds. 3) Even the auto parts store is a landmark in Medina County. The historic Fohn-Bless Store building at 1020 Eighteenth Street in Hondo manages to look dignified in spite of the incongruous sign on the front.

Hondo. The original town, now called Old D'Hanis, was about one mile east of the present town. It was another case where the settlers moved to get on the rail line. The U.S. Army had an outpost called Fort Lincoln near here from 1849 to 1852.

Dude ranching is big in this area. There are more guest ranches in Bandera County than there are here in Medina County, but the Old Gallagher Ranch founded by Irish immigrant Peter Gallagher, off State Highway 16 at the northeastern edge of Medina county, was one of the early ones.

The farms along the Medina River in eastern Medina County are irrigated by water from Lake Medina. The people here saw the possibility and the promise of irrigation very early,

1) *The oldest house in Hondo is the Fred Metzger place, built in 1876. It is a private home, not open to the public.* 2) *The little town of D'Hanis relocated when the railroad came through Medina County. The original settlement is called Old D'Hanis. One of the landmarks here is the ruin of the Saint Dominic Catholic Church, built about 1853 and abandoned in 1914.* 3) *Hondo became the county seat for Medina County in 1892 because Hondo was on the new railroad line. The county courthouse in Hondo is the only one Hondo has ever had. It was built in 1893.*

2

3

1) Medina Lake was the biggest artificial lake in Texas at one time. It is still a favorite with bass fishermen. The lake is in the northeast corner of the county. 2) The little opera house at Devine, on the Missouri Pacific rail line and Interstate Highway 35 in the southeast corner of Medina County is a national historic site. But no operas are performed here. The building is owned by a lawyer and he has it stuffed full of livestock feed. Feed is likely to be more useful here than opera would be.

and they typically brought it to reality themselves. The Medina Dam was built in 1912 by the Bexar-Medina-Atascosa County Water District Number One. The lake it impounds is a favorite of bass fishermen. There are several larger lakes now, but Medina once was the largest artificial lake in Texas. There are some petrified tracks in the bed of Hondo Creek made by a tyrannosaurus millions of years ago. They are on private property, off Farm Road 462, near the Bandera County line. There is a small fee for visiting the site.

The town of Devine, on Interstate 35 in the southeastern corner of Medina County, was established by the I.G.N. railroad and named for Thomas Jefferson Devine. He was a justice of the state supreme court and one of the railroad promoters. The Devine Opera House, on Main Street, across from the old railroad depot, is listed in the *National Register of Historic Places*.

FRIO COUNTY

The lost French explorer La Salle and the Spaniards Martin de Alarcon and the Marquis de Aguayo traveled through the area now known as Frio County. Mexican armies camped here on the way to and from battles with Texans in 1836 and in 1842. But there was not much to hold people here until the

1

2

3

1) Texas Ranger William A. A. Wallace made such a big name for himself on the frontier that they re-named the town in his honor when he settled here. The town used to be called Connally's Store. Now it is called Bigfoot. Wallace was generally known as Bigfoot Wallace. 2) Julius Tilden can tell some of the tales Bigfoot Wallace used to tell. Tilden is the custodian of the Bigfoot Wallace Museum in Bigfoot. 3) The museum is a replica of Bigfoot Wallace's old home in Bigfoot. The place is the intersection of Farm Road 462 and Farm Road 472, off Interstate 35. It is open every day except Monday. Bigfoot Wallace died in 1899 at the age of 82. He is buried in the State Cemetery in Austin.

railroads came and the underground water was discovered.

The first settlement was called Connally's Store. The Connallys apparently came about 1865. The name of their settlement was later changed to Bigfoot after Texas Ranger William A. A. (Bigfoot) Wallace came to live here. Wallace

1

1) Only the old courthouse and a few other stone ruins remain in what was once Frio Town. 2) What is left is on private property off State Highway 140 in the northwest corner of Frio County. The old Frio Town cemetery is on the other side of the highway, opposite the ghost of Frio Town. Calvin Massey apparently was the first person buried here, but this marker plainly is not original.

2

was a big and fearless man and a teller of tall tales. He became famous partly because of his exploits as a ranger in the company led by Captain Jack Hays and as commander of his own ranger company. And he became famous partly because one of his fellow rangers and good friends was John C. Duval. Wallace told good stories. Duval wrote them down. Duval's book *Adventures of Bigfoot Wallace* helped make Wallace a legend. The legend is preserved in a museum in the little town of Bigfoot. The museum is in an old school building on Main Street. It includes a replica of Bigfoot's old home. The museum is open every day except Monday, from nine to five. There is a small admission fee. Bigfoot is east of I-35 where Farm Roads 462 and 472 meet.

Frio County was created by the Texas state legislature in 1858 from parts of Bexar, Atascosa and Uvalde counties. It

1) Pearsall became a town after the I.G.N. railroad came through in 1881. The town became the county seat in 1883 and the present courthouse was built in 1905. It is rather plain for a Texas courthouse. 2) Farming is the big moneymaker in Frio County. There is no exaggeration in the claim on the base of the peanut monument here. Some years the Frio County peanut crop goes over fifty million pounds.

was not organized until 1871. The original county seat was a settlement called Frio Town. This settlement had grown up around the spot where early Spanish and Mexican travelers had been in the habit of crossing the Frio River. The place had earlier been known as the old crossing or the presidio crossing, because of the quantity of military junk that was scattered around it. Frio Town was a busy and promising place in the 1870s. There was a stone jailhouse, built in 1872, and a stone courthouse, built in 1877 after the original frame courthouse burned. There was a school, a church, a masonic lodge, and there were several homes and stores. Ranching was the main business. Those were the days of the open range, long trail drives and occasional Comanche raids.

The fencing wars and the fence law of 1884 changed the way people here lived and did business. But the biggest change came in 1881 when the I.G.N. railroad missed Frio Town on its way from San Antonio to Laredo. Most of the

The oldest building in Pearsall is the old Frio County Jail that was built immediately after the county seat moved here. Prisoners are held now in a newer building and the old jail building is a museum. It is not often open, but visitors can sometimes get somebody from the sheriff's office to show them through.

residents of Frio Town dismantled their frame homes and moved them to the new town of Pearsall on the rail line. Frio Town became a ghost town. The old rock courthouse is still standing, and the walls of the old jailhouse where Sam Bass and Frank and Jesse James supposedly once were prisoners are still standing. But they are now private property. The old courthouse and jail, one house and the old cemetery are all that is left of Frio Town. The oldest grave in the cemetery here is that of Calvin Massey, killed by Indians in 1873.

Pearsall was created by the railroad and named for a railroad man. It is also on Interstate Highway 35, so it is not likely to become a ghost town in the foreseeable future. Pearsall became the county seat of Frio County in 1883. The present courthouse was built in 1905.

One of the landmarks in Pearsall is a monument to the peanut. The county produces about 50 million pounds of peanuts a year. Oil and gas have been produced here since the 1930s, but farming and ranching still produce most of the income.

The oldest building in Pearsall is the county jail built in 1884 right after the county seat moved here. The county built a new jail in 1967 and the old jail building has been turned into a museum. The location is 600 East Medina Street, just off I-35. The exhibits include collections of articles used by the early residents of the area. There is no charge for admission, but at the last report, the old jail museum in Pearsall was open only on Saturday and Sunday afternoons.

1) A replica of the original Atascosa County Courthouse provides an office for the highway patrol in Jourdanton. 2) The present courthouse was built in 1912 when courthouse architecture was making the transition from the flamboyance of the nineties to the WPA style of the thirties.

ATASCOSA COUNTY

Atascosa County was organized in 1856. The area previously had been part of the Bexar District.

The original county seat was a settlement called Navatasco. The county government later moved to Pleasanton and then to Jourdanton. The present courthouse in Jourdanton was built in 1912. A replica of the first courthouse at Jourdanton stands at 703 Oak Street.

Atascosa County takes its name from the Atascosa River. The word atascosa means boggy in Spanish, so we can assume that the early Spanish settlers must have bogged down a few times trying to travel through this territory.

1

1) *The water tower in Poteet does its best to look like a strawberry. 2) Oil and gas and cattle earn more money here, but strawberries get the attention around Poteet. The town advertises itself as the strawberry capital of Texas. A concrete strawberry decorates the lawn in front of the city hall. 3) And the big event in Poteet is the annual strawberry festival in April with prizes for the fanciest berries. 4) The longhorns were tough. They could go two or three days without water. They were fierce enough to protect their calves from the wolves and other predators. And they could walk great distances to market without losing much weight on the way.*

2

3

Some of the earliest Spanish ranches were in this part of Texas. The missions at San Antonio had satellite communities raising livestock here and individual ranches were operating here, too, as early as the 1700s. Longhorns were roaming free all over Texas when the earliest Anglo settlers came. The longhorns evolved from the cattle the Spanish imported and these wild cows were the base the Texas cattle industry was built on. This Longhorn Museum in Pleasanton exhibits some early ranch and railroad equipment. The museum is open to the public on weekdays and there is no admission charge. Here, they claim this area was the real birthplace of the American cowboy because the vaqueros on the earliest Spanish ranches worked out the basic techniques for handling cattle from horseback.

This area was settled by Spanish and Mexican ranchers before the revolution of 1836. Oil and gas produce the biggest part of this county's income. Ranching earns more money than farming here, but farming is important.

The same factor that caused the Spanish to call this area boggy makes it good farming country. There is plenty of water. The town of Poteet in the northern part of the county calls itself the strawberry city. People here claim that forty percent of the Texas strawberry crop is grown in this immediate vicinity. There is a big monument in the shape of a strawberry on the grounds of the Poteet City Hall, and the community holds a strawberry festival every year in April. There are several commercial nurseries growing flowers at Poteet, too.

Two of the highways from San Antonio to the Mexican border pass through Atascosa County: State Highway 16, from San Antonio to Zapata passes by Poteet and through Jourdanton. And U.S. 281 from San Antonio to McAllen and Reynosa passes through Pleasanton.

87

Laredo and the Lower Border

McMullen, Duval, Jim Hogg, Starr, Zapata,
Webb, LaSalle, Dimmit counties.

This is brush country and ranch country, with some irrigated farms and some oil and gas.

There was an effort a number of years ago, when our highway system was still developing, to designate a Pan-American Highway to link Alaska and Panama. Not much is said about a Pan-American Highway, as such, anymore. But it is possible to drive from Alaska through Canada and the United States, Mexico and Central America to the Panama Canal and the logical route through this part of the world is Interstate 35, to Laredo. The interstate follows the route of old U.S. 81 and that road was part of the Pan-American Highway, in the days when the term was still in use.

More international highway travelers pass through Laredo than pass through any other city on the Texas border. It is the border city most accessible to most Texans.

The most direct route from San Antonio to Laredo is Interstate 35. But we encourage you to take State Highway 16 south to Rio Grande City and U.S. 83 to Falcon Lake and Laredo. If you want to make side trips from a comfortable base, Laredo is the place.

MCMULLEN COUNTY

A number of historic personalities passed through what is now McMullen County. But none of them stayed. A number

Samuel J. Tilden just missed being president of the United States. He got a few more votes than Rutherford B. Hayes did in 1876. But a special commission found a reason to declare Hayes the winner. Tilden had the satisfaction of having a town named for him, though. The town of Tilden is the county seat of McMullen County. The present courthouse was built in 1930.

of bandits and outlaws congregated here in the middle 1800s because the area was on the stage route between Laredo and San Antonio, and there was no law to speak of. But the population has never grown much. This is brush country and cow country.

McMullen County was originally created in 1858 from parts of Atascosa, Bexar and Live Oak counties. But there were too many outlaws and too few respectable people, and the effort to maintain a county government was abandoned in the 1860s. The county was reorganized in 1877. A little settlement on the Frio River was chosen as the county seat. The settlement had been called Rio Frio, then Dogtown, and then Colfax. The name was changed to Tilden after it became the county seat. The first county judge supposedly picked the name to honor Samuel J. Tilden. The minutes of the commissioner's court identify Tilden as president-elect of the U.S. It was wishful thinking. Tilden was the Democrats' nominee for president in the election of 1876. He was the apparent winner, but the result was disputed. A commission was established to rule on the dispute. There were eight Republicans and seven Democrats on the commission and they decided in favor of

Tilden was known as Dogtown before it was named Tilden. When the town was called Dogtown, this was the Dogtown jail. It is on the courthouse square, but it is just an office, now. The old jail was built in 1880.

Republican Rutherford B. Hayes. The vote was eight to seven.

The present courthouse was built in 1930. The county was named for John McMullen. He and James McGloin brought to Texas the Irish settlers who established San Patricio in 1831. The kind of town Tilden was, in the early days before it was named Tilden, had considerable need for a handy place to dispose of over-matched gunfighters. The old boothill cemetery filled that need. The cemetery is one block north of the courthouse.

The town of Tilden has been larger during short periods in the past than it is now. The discovery of oil in the county caused a little boom around 1920. But the population of Tilden probably never has been above a thousand. It is one of the smaller county seats in Texas.

A college was established here shortly after the outlaws were driven out. McMullen College began classes in 1881 with a Baptist minister named John Van Epps Covey in charge. The college was absorbed into the public school system in the late 1890s. The same thing happened with many of the other early private colleges in Texas.

Tilden sits on the bank of the Frio River, and it has a good

1

1) Men killed in gunfights during the frontier days were often unidentified or known only by an alias or a nickname and they were often buried in makeshift cemeteries with little ceremony. Some were buried in the boothill cemetery at Tilden. Some reputable citizens were buried here, too. But most of the markers have no names. The cemetery is one block north of the courthouse. 2) The McMullen County Museum has recently been established in an old stone store building across River Street from the courthouse. The exhibits here include a replica of a pioneer blacksmith shop. Hours of operation had not been fixed at the last report, but you can inquire at the county clerk's office if the museum is not open.

2

chance to become a resort area. The Bureau of Reclamation is building a dam in Choke Canyon on the Frio a few miles up river from the point where the Frio runs into the Nueces. The dam is over the county line in Live Oak County, and the town closest to the dam is Three Rivers in Live Oak County. But Tilden is at what will be the western end of the reservoir.

The lake development is wiping out the McMullen County town of Calliham. The town site will not actually be under water, but the Department of the Interior is taking over the site to turn it into a recreation area. There will be campsites

Someone with too little to do has been taking pot shots at the historical marker recording the ambush of the Thomas Stringfield family. The marker is on Farm Road 624 about 24 miles southwest of Tilden. The actual attack occurred about 5½ miles northwest of this spot, in the fall of 1870. The Stringfields' eight-year-old daughter survived the attack.

here eventually. About twenty of the families being uprooted by the development are planning to establish a new Calliham a couple of miles south of the present site.

No area is deliberately flooded these days without a careful effort to identify and catalog any valuable sites or artifacts there may be in the area. The Bureau of Reclamation has had archaeologists studying Choke Canyon for more than four years. They have located several hundred buried Indian campsites, bones and arrowheads, plus a few pioneer cemeteries and the remains of some pioneer homesteads. The archaeologists believe the evidence proves humans were living in this area ten thousand years ago. Presumably some of these artifacts will be on display some day at the reservoir. State Highway 72 between Three Rivers and Tilden is being re-located to follow the south shore of the reservoir. State Highway 16 runs north and south right through the middle of McMullen County and intersects State Highway 72 at Tilden. U.S. 59 cuts across the southeastern corner of the county but passes nowhere near any town in McMullen County.

The Comanche and Apache Indians continued to harass the settlers in this area up into the 1870s. There is a marker at a roadside rest stop on Farm Road 624, about one mile west of State Highway 16, recording one of the last such incidents. The marker recalls that it was near here in September of 1870 that the Stringfield family was ambushed by a mixed party of Indians and Mexican bandits. Thomas Stringfield and his wife Sara were killed. Their two young sons were kidnapped, and little Ida Alice Stringfield was stabbed several times and

1) Headquarters of the Duchy of Duval was the courthouse at San Diego, built in 1916. The first railroad in the county missed the town by seven miles. So, San Diego just picked up and moved to the railroad in 1876. 2) Federal Judge Thomas Duval was one of the three brothers the county was named for. The other brothers were Burr Duval, executed by the Mexicans in the Goliad massacre, and Bigfoot Wallace's writing friend, John C. Duval.

left for dead. Ida was just eight years old at the time. She survived, and when she grew up she tried to trace her two brothers. A man showed up in 1908 claiming that he was the missing Tommy Stringfield. He had a granite marker put up at the site of the Stringfield graves with an inscription saying, "Thomas Stringfield, killed by Indians, September 28, 1870, Sarah Stringfield killed by Indians, September 28, 1870, erected by Tommy Stringfield (Two Braids) 1909." This man said Two Braids was the name the Indians gave him. But his story was never verified, and Ida considered him an impostor. She married William Hatfield and lived in Medina until she died in 1937. Her children had a marker put up at the Stringfield gravesite to contradict the claim made on the marker put up by the man who said he was Tommy Stringfield. Their marker includes the notation, "Two Braids who performed with a wild west show to raise money for the headstones here was proved an impostor by the only survivor of the slaughter, Ida Alice Stringfield Hatfield."

DUVAL COUNTY

Duval County was named for a distinguished family of early settlers, but it is better known as the home of a family named Parr. Duval County was named for the family of Burr

Duval County got most of its fame from three people named Parr. Members of the Parr family dominated politics in the area for three generations. Newspaper writers called them the Dukes of Duval. The first duke was Archie Parr. He was a school teacher and a cowboy and a ranch foreman before he went into politics. He was one of the most influential members of the state senate for many years before he died in 1942.

H. Duval when it was organized from parts of Starr, Live Oak and Nueces counties in 1858.

Burr Duval came to Texas from Kentucky in 1835 to fight in the Texas Revolution. He and his brother John joined James Fannin's little army at Goliad in time to be captured by Mexican General José Urrea at the Battle of Coleto. Burr Duval was executed by the Mexican troops in the Goliad massacre. John somehow escaped and lived to write about his adventures in a series of articles called "Early Times in Texas." John also wrote *The Adventures of Bigfoot Wallace* about the life of his friend and fellow Texas Ranger William A. A. Wallace. J. Frank Dobie ranked John C. Duval as Texas' first man of letters. Another Duval brother named Thomas moved to Texas after the revolution and served as a federal judge before and after the Civil War. The Duval brothers were the sons of William P. Duval. He served as a member of Congress and as a federal judge before he followed his sons to Texas in 1848. The senior Duval settled at Galveston and started a law practice. Sam Houston was one of his clients.

None of the Duvals apparently ever lived in Duval County, and it probably never occurred to any of them that there someday would be somebody known as the Duke of Duval. But somebody was.

The title probably was invented by a newspaper writer or an envious politician. It was first applied to Archie Parr sometime in the 1920s and later inherited by Archie's son, George. The Parrs controlled politics in Duval and Jim Wells counties for three generations, from their ranch headquarters

The third duke's political career was de-railed by federal authorities and the courts. Archer Parr was convicted of perjury. He was a nephew of the second duke. The second duke was George Parr, best remembered for the role he played in helping Lyndon Johnson win the close contest for U.S. Senator in 1948.

at Benavides. Archie started out as a hired hand on a ranch. Then he got elected county commissioner and then state senator. He died in 1942. George Parr became county judge and a power in Texas democratic party politics. One of his precincts produced the eighty-seven votes that made Lyndon Johnson the winner of the bitter race with Coke Stevenson for the U.S. Senate in 1948. Parr delivered favors. His Mexican-American constituents delivered votes. George Parr was eventually tripped up by the Internal Revenue Service and changing standards of political conduct. He was convicted of evading income taxes in 1974, and he killed himself on the ranch at Benavides in 1975.

George Parr's nephew, Archer Parr, tried to follow in the footsteps of Archie and George. Archer got elected county judge, but then he was convicted on a federal charge of perjury. There are no Parrs in office here now, and their influence seems to be ebbing.

The county seat of Duval County has been the town of San Diego from the beginning. The town was founded in 1858 about the same time the county was organized. San Diego has moved since then, though. It was originally about seven miles from the present site. The town moved in 1876 to get on the route of the Corpus Christi, San Diego and Rio Grande Railroad. The railroad reached the town in 1879. The present courthouse was built in 1916.

The name of the town of San Diego was applied to a plot to foment trouble between the United States and Mexico in 1915 and 1916. Germany was suspected of being involved in the plot. The "Plan of San Diego" was a plan for an uprising of

Many of the ranches in Duval County are the kind that must be rated the best kind. They are the kind producing both cattle and oil, in the best Texas tradition.

Mexican-American and black citizens of the United States to coincide with Mexican attacks across the border into Texas. There were some raids and other incidents, but none of them occurred in San Diego, and there never was any real uprising by the black and Mexican-American citizens of Texas. But the incidents probably hastened the United States entry into World War I against the Germans.

San Diego remains the largest city in Duval County, but it is not on a major highway. U.S. 59 and Texas Highway 16 both pass through Freer, so Freer is probably the town most travelers see in this county.

Freer did not become a town until about 1907 when oil was discovered in the area. The town was named for the owner of the land where the town was established. He was O. J. Freer.

The chief income of Duval County comes from oil, but cattle ranches are also important here.

JIM HOGG COUNTY

Jim Hogg County was organized in 1913 from parts of Brooks and Duval counties. The county was named for former Governor James Stephen Hogg.

The area was settled first by Mexican and Spanish ranchers in the late eighteenth century. It is still mostly ranch country

1

People were living in the area that is now Jim Hogg County as early as the 1700s. But Jim Hogg County was not organized until 1913. Hebbronville is the county seat and it is older than the county is. The town was established in 1881. 1) This courthouse was built in 1913. The county was named for the first native Texan to be elected governor of the state. 2) The Texas Historical Commission has authorized a marker for the old house built by Bonifacio Garza. It is now a private residence. 3) The little settlement of Randado is far older than the county or the county seat. Randado was headquarters for a Mexican ranch established in 1836. Oil now produces more income than cattle in this county.

2

3

with some oil and gas production.

The county seat is Hebbronville. The town was established in 1881 by W. R. Hebbron as a stop on the Texas-Mexican Railroad. This little town shipped more cattle than any other town in the United States in the period between 1917 and 1928. The present courthouse was built in 1913.

1) A skirmish between Mexican bandits and a unit of the U.S. Eighth Cavalry at Randado in 1891 attracted more attention than it probably deserved. Richard Harding Davis happened to be traveling with the cavalry. He was one of the ranking newspaper correspondents of the time. No military skirmish is minor if a major writer is present. 2) The little Catholic church at Randado is a registered Texas landmark. Randado is on State Highway 16 in western Jim Hogg County.

The little settlement of Randado, on State Highway 16 south of Hebbronville, is much older than the county seat. Randado was established about 1836 as the center of a ranch the Mexican government granted to Jose´ Policarpo Rodri´gues.

Randado was the scene of a minor skirmish between the U.S. Army and forces led by the Mexican bandit Catarino Garza in 1891. Garza and his followers camped outside the town. The U.S. Eighth Cavalry was sent out from Laredo to chase Garza off. Garza skipped out, and there was no battle. There might not have been any notice taken of the maneuver at all except that the noted journalist, Richard Harding Davis, was traveling with the Eighth Cavalry.

There is an old Catholic church in Randado on Farm Road 496.

Jim Hogg County is without any major highways. The most traveled route in the county is the road from San Antonio to Zapata, State Highway 16. It passes through both Hebbronville and Randado.

Dr. J. H. Starr came to Texas in 1837 and got active in public affairs right away. He was secretary of the treasury under President Mirabeau Lamar and he later helped run the Confederate postal system during the Civil War. Dr. Starr lived most of his life in east Texas and he died in Marshall in 1890. There is no evidence that he ever set foot in this part of the state. But this county was named for him when it was organized in 1848.

STARR COUNTY

Starr County was organized in 1848 from part of the original Nueces County. It was named for Dr. J. H. Starr. He was secretary of the treasury during the days of the Republic.

The county seat is Rio Grande City on the Rio Grande. The city and the surrounding area were part of the colony established by Jose´ de Escandon´ in 1753 during the days of Spanish rule. The town that became Rio Grande City was founded by Henry Clay Davis. He called the original settlement here Rancho Davis, and he developed a river port that prospered through and beyond the Civil War years. Dams and other changes along the border river have changed the flow so that the Rio Grande is no longer navigable at this point.

General Zachary Taylor established a military post here in 1848 during the war between the United States and Mexico after Texas joined the union. The post was originally called Camp Ringgold, in honor of Major David Ringgold. He was one of the first American casualties in the war with Mexico, killed in the Battle of Palo Alto. The camp later became known as Ringgold Barracks, and the name was changed to Fort Ringgold in 1878 when the original temporary buildings were replaced by permanent buildings of stone, brick and frame. The army maintained the fort until 1944 and then turned it over to the Rio Grande Independent School District. Part of the old fort is now part of the campus of the Rio Grande City High School. There is a new high school building on the grounds, but some classes also are held in the old cavalry barracks. Robert E. Lee was here before the Civil

1) General Zachary Taylor established the military post in Rio Grande City that eventually became Fort Ringgold. Taylor led the U.S. armies in the war with Mexico that followed Texas' annexation to the union. 2) This fort was named for Major David Ringgold, one of the casualties of the Mexican War. It is now the property of the Rio Grande School District.

2

War when he was commander of the U.S. Army's Department of Texas. Fort Ringgold is off U.S. Highway 83 at the eastern city limits of Rio Grande City. The present courthouse in Rio Grande City was built in 1938 and remodeled in 1976.

Highway 83 is the principal highway in Starr County. It follows the Rio Grande from La Grulla on the east to Falcon Village on the west. There are toll bridges across the Rio Grande into Mexico from Rio Grande City to the Mexican Ciudad Camargo, and from Roma los Saenz to the Mexican city of Miguel Aleman.

Also on the south side of the river, opposite Roma, is Ciudad Mier. Mier has never been a city of much consequence, but it occupies a sizable place in Texas history. A party of Texas adventurers staged an unauthorized raid into Mexico during the early days of the Republic of Texas. They briefly occupied Laredo and Guerrero, but their leaders decided in December of 1842 that they had done all the

1) Starr County has one of those thirties-model courthouses. The courthouse at Rio Grande City was built in 1938 and remodeled in 1976. 2) Smugglers have been thriving on this section of the border for generations and they still are. There are uncounted unofficial crossing points on the river here and three official crossings. The international toll bridge at Rio Grande City is one of them.

damage they could do. So they called off the expedition. But some of the men declined to be called off. They moved on down the river on their own and attacked Mier. The Mexican army was waiting for them. There was a battle. The Mexicans won, and 176 of the Texans were captured. Most of them were released eventually, but President Santa Anna ordered some of them to be executed. The prisoners were required to draw beans from a container that held 159 white beans and seventeen black beans. The seventeen men drawing black beans were shot. One of the leaders of the Texas expedition was Ewen Cameron. He drew a white bean, but Santa Anna changed the rules and had him shot anyway.

Texans fought in Mexico again, with the U.S. Army, during the Mexican War in 1846. And there were some skirmishes between outlaws and troops after that. But the border

1) Camargo is one of the oldest cities on either side of the border. It was the first settlement founded by the Spanish colonizer Jose de Escandon in 1749. 2) The Spanish settlers here called their town Bueno Vista and later they called it Garcia's Ranch. A priest visiting the settlement in the 1830s suggested it should be called Roma because he thought the hills resembled those in Rome. It has been Roma ever since. Our Lady of Refuge Church here dates from 1854. The sanctuary has been rebuilt, but the steeple is original.

1

2

between Texas and Mexico has been peaceful now for more than fifty years, and crossing the border is an uncomplicated exercise. U.S. citizens need no passport, visa or tourist card to visit a Mexican bordertown. Just tell the Mexican official at the border that you are only going to visit the border city. And returning to the U.S. side, citizens only need to say they are citizens and declare anything they have bought in Mexico. The value of Mexican goods a traveler can bring across the border without paying duty varies from time to time. Ask what the limit is before you go across. Each adult traveler can bring one quart of liquor into the U.S. without any U.S. duty. But there is a Texas state tax on all alcoholic beverages brought across the border, and there is also a state law forbidding the importation into Texas of anything alcoholic in containers smaller than a half pint. There are miniature bottles of almost anything you can think of for sale in Mexico. But they will be confiscated if you try to bring them into Texas.

1

1) Steamboats could travel up the Rio Grande this far in the earlier days before the dams were built. Roma was a port. The people here grew very prosperous and they built some substantial buildings. This classic building was used for several commercial purposes before Dr. Mario Ramirez acquired it in 1959 and converted it to a hospital. The Manuel Ramirez Memorial Hospital operated here until it moved to new quarters recently. This building was built in the 1840s and it is still standing at the northwest corner of the plaza in Roma. 2) This house is on the plaza near the old steamboat landing in Roma. It is known as the Noah Cox house but Cox was not the original owner. This house apparently was built in the 1850s.

2

If you are going farther into Mexico than the bordertowns, you will need a tourist card. You can get one from the immigration authorities at the border or at the Mexican consulates and Mexican government tourist offices in major cities on this side of the border. If you are driving your car into Mexico, even to the border cities, you need Mexican insurance. You can and should buy it at the border. You don't need to worry about exchanging money. The Mexicans will accept U.S. currency for anything they have for sale.

No border town south of the Rio Grande looks any more Latin than the town of Roma on the Texas side of the river. Part of the movie *Viva Zapata* was made here. Roma was settled in the 1760s as part of the original Jose´de Escandon´ colony. This, too, was a riverport before the flow of the river was altered.

1

2

1) The Texas town of Roma resembles a Mexican town so much that the producers of the movie "Viva Zapata" used it in the 1950s as a setting for their film about the Mexican rebel. This is the old Guerra building, built in 1834 as a combination store and residence. 2) This building may remind the traveler of New Orleans. There is a reason. The iron balcony railing was designed and made in New Orleans and shipped here. This was a home until it was acquired recently by the Knights of Columbus. 3) The Ramirez house was built in 1857 by Jose' Maria Garcia. The Ramirez family acquired it in the early 1900s. The house overlooks the river and the city of Miguel Aleman on the Mexican side.

3

1) The Roma Historical Museum has an assortment of pioneer vehicles, implements and tools on display. There is no admission fee, but donations are encouraged. 2) An international toll bridge across the Rio Grande links Roma with two border cities on the Mexican side.

Most of the buildings here now were built in the years right after the Civil War with money made from trade and smuggling. Fifteen blocks of Roma have been listed in the *National Register of Historic Places*. Buildings in the historic district include Our Lady of Refuge Church on the Main Plaza, and the convent at the northeast corner of the plaza. Also on the plaza is the old Guerra Building. This is a combination commercial and residential building designed by the German architect Heinrich Portscheller and built in 1834.

The Noah Cox house on River Street, just off U.S. 83, was built in the 1850s, along European lines. The Ramirez Building on River Street was built in 1857 by Jose' Garcia.

1) The ancient Mexican city of Mier is on the south bank of the Rio Grande opposite Roma. Some freewheeling adventurers from the Republic of Texas were captured by Mexican troops in Mier in 1842 and Santa Anna had some of them executed. 2) Mexican Highway 2 runs northward from Miguel Aleman, opposite Roma, to Nuevo Laredo and southward to Reynosa and Matamoros. You should have tourist cards, Mexican car insurance and proof of ownership of your car if you are going this far. 3) The Falcon Dam and Reservoir on the Rio Grande is part of an effort to control flooding on the border river. There is a state park on the Texas side.

The Knights of Columbus Hall at Estrella Street and Zaragoza Alley was built in 1884 as a home, and it was known as the Pink House. There is a small museum in the old building at Estrella and Lincoln. It is open weekdays. Donations are welcome.

The site of Mission Mier a Vista is about three and a half miles northwest of Roma on U.S. 83, on the way to Falcon Dam.

The Falcon State Park at the lower end of Falcon Reservoir on the Rio Grande is one of the state's Class I parks. There is

1) The county seat of Zapata County is an old town settled originally by the Spanish in 1770. The Spanish name of the town was Carrizo, but Texans changed it to Zapata in 1858. The courthouse is a relatively new one, built in 1953. 2) Most of the shoreline on the U.S. side of Falcon Lake is in Zapata County. But the dam and the state park are in Starr County. Falcon is noted for big catfish and black bass.

an entry fee of two dollars per vehicle unless you have an annual permit. (The entrance fee went up from a dollar per vehicle in September of 1978, and the annual permit went up at the same time from twelve to fifteen dollars.)

The Falcon State Park has eighty-six campsites and twenty-four screened shelters for rent. There are additional charges for the campsites and shelters. The address for reservations is Box 2, Falcon Heights, Texas 78545. The phone number is 512-848-5327.

There is a free border crossing at the Falcon Dam leading to the Mexican city of Nuevo Guerro.

ZAPATA COUNTY

The present Zapata County was another outgrowth of the Spanish colony Jose de Escandon established on the Rio

1

1) *Some ancient settlements on both sides of the river were flooded when the International Boundary and Water Commission built the Falcon dam on the Rio Grande. 2) State agencies and the National Park Service compiled an inventory of the real estate that was submerged, complete with photographs, floor plans and descriptions.*

2

Grande in 1750. The county was created in 1858 from parts of Webb and Starr counties.

The first settlement was Hacienda de Dolores, near the present town of San Ygnacio. The county is part of the area the Mexicans continued to claim after the Texas Revolution. Mexico claimed the boundary between Mexico and Texas was the Nueces River, and this claim was the main issue in the war between the United States and Mexico after Texas joined the United States. The treaty ending the war fixed the boundary at the Rio Grande where Texans had always claimed it was.

Zapata County apparently was named for Colonel Antonio Zapata. He was a rich and prominent Mexican resident of Guerrero on the Mexican side of the Rio Grande. Zapata and General Antonio Canales were among the leaders of a brief effort to create a republic on the Rio Grande, including parts of south Texas and northern Mexico. They were defeated by the forces of the Mexican government, and Colonel Zapata was executed.

There is more about the Republic of the Rio Grande in the

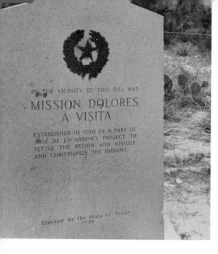

1) The earliest settlers in this area were Spanish colonists brought in by José de Escandón. Their first settlement was a little mission about 12 miles north of the present town of San Ygnacio. Little is left at the site except the marker the state put up in 1936. 2) The oldest building still standing in the old town of San Ygnacio is the Jesús Treviño House at Treviño and Uribe streets. This house is a recorded Texas landmark. It was built about 1830.

section on Webb County.

The original site of Dolores is listed in the *National Register of Historic Places*. There is not anything left at the site except the ruins of a stone house and some fragments of foundations. The site is twenty-six miles north of Zapata on U.S. 83.

Most of the town of San Ygnacio is also in the *National Register of Historic Places*. The oldest structure standing here is the Jesús Treviño House, built about 1830. The Treviño House is at the corner of Treviño and Uribe streets. The last

James Webb was sent to Mexico in 1841 to be the Minister for the Republic of Texas. But he didn't stay. The Mexicans refused to accept him. So Webb ran for the Texas Senate, instead, and served four years. He had come to Texas from Florida in 1838. He gave up a federal judgeship to come here. He was a district judge in Corpus Christi when he died in 1856. The Legislature had named Webb County for him eight years earlier, in 1848.

recorded armed invasion of the United States occurred here at San Ygnacio in June of 1916. A band of Mexicans made a raid here, and the ensuing fight killed around a dozen people. The raid was a by-product of the German attempt to generate trouble between Mexico and the United States.

The county seat of Zapata County is the town of Zapata. The town was originally called Carrizo when it was settled by Spanish and Mexican farmers in the 1770s. The name was changed when the county was organized. The present courthouse was built in 1953.

The railroads never discovered Zapata, and it remained a rather isolated community until the highway system was developed. There is some oil production here and some gas, but farming and ranching are the main occupations.

The atmosphere and the architecture here were colonial Spanish until the Falcon Dam was completed in 1952.

Settlements on both sides of the river had been damaged by floods repeatedly, from 1751 onward. So the governments of Mexico and the United States established an international boundary and water commission in 1944 to work on plans to control the floods on the Rio Grande. They decided upon a series of three dams. Two of them have been built. It is doubtful the third one will be built because many environmental groups are against it. That third one was supposed to be the upper dam. The middle dam in the planned series is Amistad, in Val Verde County. This one, in Zapata County, is the lower one and the first one completed. It has changed the character of the area by attracting fishing enthusiasts and tourists to what had been a distinctly rural area. Some of the oldest buildings in the area were flooded by the reservoir.

Laredo is the county seat for Webb County and the city was already old when the county was organized. Laredo was old even when the Battle of San Jacinto was fought. The city was established in 1755. The present courthouse was built in 1909.

The University of Texas, the National Park Service and the Texas Historical Foundation made an attempt to preserve some record of the culture that was here before the lake. Notes and photographs have been compiled and published in a booklet called *Historic Architecture of Texas — The Falcon Reservoir* by the Texas Historical Commission and the Texas Historical Foundation.

The Falcon State Park is across the county line in Starr County. The reservoir was named for the little village of Falcon, and the village apparently was named for an early explorer by the name of Miguel de la Garza Falcon.

Anglers can fish around the ruins of the old Mexican town of Guerrero on the south shore of Falcon Reservoir. Most of the town is flooded. Most of the residents moved to the new town of Guerrero, a little farther south, but a few still live here in what is left of old Guerrero.

WEBB COUNTY

The area that is now Webb County is part of the territory settled by Jose de Escandon in 1755. The county was organized in 1848 from part of Bexar County. It was named for lawyer James Webb. He came to Texas after the revolution. He served as secretary of the treasury, secretary of state and as attorney general during the days of the Republic. He also served in the Congress during the days of the Republic and then became a district judge in Corpus Christi after Texas joined the Union.

It is popularly supposed that Texas has been under six flags. It is a slight exaggeration since the French never did seriously claim the area. But in Laredo, they count all six, plus one more. They count seven flags here because the city was part of the territory claimed briefly by the Republic of the Rio Grande. Mexican federalists met in this house in the old section of Laredo in 1840 to proclaim the republic, but it never was much more than proclaimed. The federalists didn't have the muscle to hold the big areas of Texas and Mexico they claimed. The house is now a museum.

The city of Laredo has been the county seat of Webb County since the county was organized. The present courthouse was built in 1909. The city is much older than the county. The city was eighty-one years old when President Santa Anna of Mexico came through here in 1836 on his way to San Antonio to punish the rebels who had seized the Alamo. Laredo was Mexican. There was no particular sentiment here in favor of the Anglo revolution. So the citizens of Laredo staged a ball in honor of Santa Anna when he stopped here. Sentiment against the Santa Anna regime increased later on. And Laredo was the headquarters of the Mexican federalist party in the late 1830s. The federalists held a convention in Laredo in January of 1840 and wrote a declaration of independence. The government of Mexico, at the time, was still disputing the Texas claim that Texas extended to the Rio Grande. Mexico claimed the boundary was the Nueces River. The federalists claimed that their Republic of the Rio Grande included the disputed territory between the Nueces and the Rio Grande and all of New Mexico and the Mexican states of Tamaulipas, Coahuila, Nuevo León, Zacatecas, Durango and Chihuahua. The convention was held and the declaration was written in a little building on Zaragoza Street overlooking the Rio Grande. The building is still here. It is a museum now, and La Posada Motel is right next door.

The independence declared here was never achieved. The

1) The U.S. Army's old Fort McIntosh is now a museum and campus. 2) The old Commissary warehouse and three other original buildings on the grounds of the old fort have been restored to house the Nuevo Santander Museum. The commissary warehouse is the oldest building here. 3) The old original central district of Laredo is the last example of an extant settlement on the north bank of the Rio Grande founded during the Escandon colonization.

1

1) San Augustine Plaza takes its name from the San Augustine Church, facing the plaza at 214 South St. Augustine Street. This is the oldest church in Laredo. 2) One of the surviving Spanish-style buildings in the Laredo historic district is the Casa Ortiz. It is at 915 Zaragoza Street.

2

small army of the Republic of the Rio Grande was led by General Antonio Canales and Colonel Antonio Zapata. Zapata was captured in the first battle with Santa Anna's forces, and he was executed. Canales was captured about eight months later and persuaded to change sides. He became an officer in Santa Anna's army, and that was the end of the Republic of the Rio Grande. But Laredo remained a Mexican town.

The new Republic of Texas made no real effort to enforce its claim to this territory until Texas joined the Union. Then General Zachary Taylor brought the U.S. Army to the disputed territory. War began in 1846 and a force commanded by former Texas President Mirabeau Lamar occupied Laredo.

The U.S. Army established a fort at Laredo as soon as the war with Mexico ended. It was named Fort McIntosh, and it continued to be a U.S. Army post until 1946, except for the

1) *Shoppers in Nuevo Laredo are pretty likely to wind up on Guerrero Avenue. The shops are concentrated along this street and here also is the main market where meat, produce and all kinds of souvenirs are offered for sale. It is considered good form to haggle over prices. It is expected.*
2) *Some of the objects offered for sale here are made while you wait. This woman is creating an artistic piece of glassware.*

period when Confederate troops took it over during the Civil War.

The Laredo Junior College and Texas A & I University now occupy part of the grounds of the old fort. The surviving army buildings are now part of the Nuevo Santander Museum, at the west end of Washington Street.

The ruins of the original earthworks built in 1850 are still visible here, too. The museum is open every weekday and on Saturday and Sunday afternoons. It is free. The fort and museum are listed in the *National Register of Historic Places,* and so is the old downtown section of Laredo.

The buildings displaying state historical markers here include the Casa Ortiz at 915 Zaragoza, and the San Augustine Church at 214 S. St. Augustine Street. This is the oldest church in Laredo.

The first railroad reached Laredo in 1881. The city has been a tourist resort ever since. It is one of the major ports of entry on the border between the United States and Mexico.

The Mexican city of Nuevo Laredo, on the south bank of

The most elegant shop on the Avenida Guerrero may be the most elegant on the border. Marti's is just a couple of blocks from the south end of the old bridge in Nuevo Laredo. Unusual textiles, furnishings and decorative items are the specialties here. The bargaining over prices that is accepted as normal in the market and most of the souvenir shops usually does not work very well in the better shops. But sometimes it does work at Marti's. You might start by asking if there is a discount for cash.

the Rio Grande, has grown to a population of around 200,000. The two Laredos were connected by a ferry until 1889 when the first bridge was built. There are two modern international toll bridges today. Tourists move back and forth freely. Many of the citizens of Mexico prefer to buy their staples and clothing in Laredo, on the Texas side. The shops and markets in Nuevo Laredo, on the Mexican side, are crowded with shoppers from the United States, buying clothes, pottery, tiles, furniture, jewelry and decorative items.

If you drive your own car across the border, you should have Mexican insurance, and you need to remember that Mexican authorities take a more serious view of traffic accidents than most of us are used to. But many thousands of U.S. citizens drive around Mexico every year without having any of the unpleasant experiences you may have heard about. Border visitors interested in shopping for more than the usual souvenirs should visit Marti's at the corner of Guerrero and Victoria streets in Nuevo Laredo. El Rio Motel on the southern edge of the city, on the highway to Monterrey, is a comfortable place to stay with good food and good service.

The Mexican National Railway runs a passenger train from Nuevo Laredo to Mexico City every day. This is the Aztec Eagle. It leaves Nuevo Laredo every evening at 6:55 and

Bullfights are not staged with any great regularity in Nuevo Laredo. You are more likely to encounter the charreada. This is a Mexican-style rodeo. The Mexicans are second to no one in horsemanship. The charreada is a regular feature of the Washington's Birthday celebration here each winter.

arrives in Mexico City twenty-five hours later. The train has old fashioned pullman cars and a diner. And the price is right. The trip in a lower berth costs about twenty-one dollars each way.

The big event here in the two Laredos every year is the celebration of Washington's birthday in February. The celebration, on both sides of the border, lasts for four days. It has been going on since 1898.

LA SALLE COUNTY

This county is on the edge of the area claimed by both the Republic of Texas and Mexico between the end of the Texas Revolution in 1836 and the end of the Mexican War in 1848. The Nueces River runs diagonally through La Salle County, and the county seat is right on the river. The Mexicans used to claim the Nueces was the northern boundary of Mexico. Texans claimed everything southward to the Rio Grande.

La Salle County was established by the legislature of the state of Texas in 1858, but the organization was not completed until 1880. The county was named for the French explorer Rene Robert Cavelier, Sieur de La Salle. La Salle

Rene Robert Cavelier traveled down the Mississippi to the Gulf of Mexico in 1682. He named the new lands he discovered Louisiana and he claimed them for the French king. This earned him the title Sieur de La Salle and the authority to establish a French colony at the mouth of the Mississippi. La Salle got lost on his way back over from France. He lost two of his ships and the other two made a crash landing on the shores of Matagorda Bay in Spanish Texas. La Salle wandered around for two years, trying to find the Mississippi until his men finally killed him. He wandered this far west on one occasion and that alarmed the Spanish and gave the Texas legislature an excuse to name this county for him when it was created much later, in 1858.

unintentionally spent the last two years of his life in Texas. He landed on the shores of Matagorda Bay in 1685 while trying to find the mouth of the Mississippi.

He has a larger place in Texas history than his accomplishments in Texas can explain. This is mostly because the Spanish thought he was trying to claim this territory for France. But all the evidence indicates La Salle spent most of his time in Texas trying to find his way to Louisiana.

The claim that Texas has been under six flags hangs on the romantic, and probably mistaken, notion that La Salle was waving the Fleur de Lis around and trying to claim Texas for his king. He had bigger problems than that. His soldiers got tired of marching around looking for Louisiana and killed La Salle, in 1687, near the present city of Navasota. He was pretty thoroughly confused about his directions, enough so that he wandered as far west as the area now called La Salle County. This probably was one reason why the Spaniards were not convinced he was really looking for the Mississippi. The man the county seat was named for came here intentionally and he was here for a long time. The county seat is Cotulla. The original settlement in La Salle County grew up around the place where the old Spanish road from Laredo to San Antonio crossed the Nueces in the southern end of the county, about where Caiman Creek runs into the Nueces. The U.S. Army established a post at this site in 1852 to protect the road. The post was named Fort Ewell, but it never was much of a fort, and it was abandoned in 1854. There is a marker at

1

2

1) The greatest roundup of wild mustang horses in history is said to have been conducted here at Cotulla in the late 1800s. A thousand horses were caught and shipped off to Argentina. This town became the county seat of La Salle County in 1882 and the present courthouse was built in 1931. 2) The county seat of the county named for a Frenchman who never lived here is named for a Polish rancher who lived here a long time. Joseph Cotulla was the first settler. He started ranching here in the 1860s when there were still herds of wild cows and horses here. The town on the Nueces River was named for Cotulla in 1882.

the site, twenty-five miles southeast of Cotulla off Farm Road 468.

An immigrant from Poland named Joe Cotulla settled here in the 1860s and started ranching. There were herds of wild cows and wild mustang horses here then. William and Amanda Burke established the La Mott ranch a little later, and other settlers began moving to this part of the frontier. The settlement that grew up around where Fort Ewell had been was named La Salle when the county was established. That settlement was the original county seat. The county seat was moved to a new site on the Nueces in 1882, and the new settlement was named Cotulla in honor of the first settler. The present courthouse in Cotulla was built in 1931.

The first railroad here was the International & Great

1) *The late President Lyndon Johnson spent some time teaching school in the early part of his career. And the first place he taught was here in Cotulla. He taught one semester at the Welhausen Elementary School.*
2) *Johnson made an appearance here once while he was President of the United States and the school board renamed the school in Johnson's honor, but it is still called Welhausen School.*

PRESIDENT
LYNDON BAINES JOHNSON
TAUGHT HERE IN
1928 – 1929

Northern, and it brought some changes. This is brush country. There is not much rainfall. It was good for ranching but not much good for farming until the I.G.N. discovered some fine sources of underground water. The railroad was interested in water for its locomotive boilers, but there was more than enough for that, and landowners began irrigating their fields. The town of Artesia Wells south of Cotulla took its name from the I.G.N. water wells. Cotulla, Artesia Wells and Encinal all were stops on the original I.G.N. rail line, now the Missouri Pacific. All three towns are also on the main highway from San Antonio to Laredo. This is Interstate 35, part of the Pan-American Highway.

The early settlers had plenty of problems with outlaws and Indians. The last Indian raid in the county was in 1878.

Cotulla's chief claim to fame probably is the fact that it is the place where the late President Lyndon B. Johnson first taught school. Johnson spent part of the year of 1929 teaching classes in the Welhausen Elementary School that still stands here.

1) The first courthouse in Dimmit County was built in the original settlement of Carrizo Springs in 1884. The building was enlarged and remodeled in 1926 and most of the original sandstone was used in the rebuilding. 2) The old horse trough that was a standard fixture on every courthouse square was preserved when the old courthouse was remodeled and it is still here today. It does not appear to have been used much recently, but the "No parking" sign seems to suggest it is still reserved for thirsty horses.

DIMMIT COUNTY

This is part of the Texas winter garden. Dimmit County was organized in 1858 from parts of Bexar, Maverick, Uvalde and Webb counties. The man the county was named for just missed being one of the martyrs of the Alamo.

Philip Dimitt was one of the early Anglo settlers in Texas. He came here from Kentucky in 1822 at the age of twenty-one. He married a Mexican citizen and took Mexican citizenship. But he joined the revolution, and he was in command of the Texas forces at Goliad briefly in 1835. Dimitt was at the Alamo in early 1836. Then he was assigned to Lavaca Bay to be public storekeeper for the Texas revolutionary army. He left the Alamo on February 23 to take over that job. It was the same day Santa Anna started his siege of the Alamo.

1) Artesian wells discovered in the 1880s provided the irrigation water that turned some of these ranchlands into very productive farms. This well at Asherton spewed water five and a half feet above the casing when it was first completed. 2) The artesian wells were discovered originally by the railroads, but the management of the water supply afterward made this county one of the centers of irrigated vegetable farming.

Santa Anna overwhelmed the garrison of the Alamo on March 6, and all the defenders were killed. Dimitt escaped that fate, but he did not outlive the Alamo garrison by very much. Mexican raiders captured him at Corpus Christi in 1841 and took him off to Mexico. Dimitt apparently committed suicide while he was a prisoner of the Mexicans.

The Texas legislature decided seventeen years later to name this border county for Dimitt, and the legislature made a mistake. The bill creating the county misspelled Dimitt's name, and the county has been Dimmit County ever since.

The first two or three attempts to settle this area failed. A black pioneer named John Townsend brought a small party of settlers here from Nacogdoches. They settled near the present town of Catarina on the old Spanish road that ran from Nacogdoches to the Rio Grande. But the Indians ran them off.

The first permanent Anglo settlement in Dimmit County was established in 1865. Several families settled on the banks of Pena and Pendencia creeks. They called their town Carrizo Springs. Carrizo is the Spanish word for reed, and the name seemed appropriate because of the stands of reeds growing along the creeks. Water was not plentiful in Dimmit County, though. So the early settlers raised more livestock than crops until the 1890s when they discovered that there is water under the ground here. The artesian wells have made Dimmit County a major producer of vegetables. An artesian well is a well

1) Vegetables from Dimmit County are shipped to produce dealers all over the country. 2) The oldest church in Carrizo Springs is the First Baptist, started in 1888 and finished in 1891. 3) Our Lady of Guadalupe Church here resembles a Spanish mission. But it was completed in 1952. 4) Espantosa is a natural lake and it was a natural camping spot in the pioneer days, but it was not a popular one. There were several Indian skirmishes here and some people thought the place was haunted by the spirits of departed warriors. Espantosa is a Spanish word that means ghost.

1

2

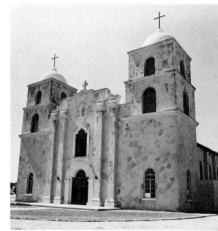

3

1

1) The Chaparral Wildlife Management Area is named for this personable bird, also called a roadrunner or "paisano." 2) The town of Catarina is an example of one of those real estate promotions that did not quite come off. Catarina is still a town. About 300 people live here. But there once were 2500 people here. The Great Depression came along just in time to short-circuit whatever hope Catarina had of becoming a garden spot. 3) This building served as a clubhouse during the time the real estate speculators were promoting the town of Catarina.

2

3

drilled into any formation where underground pressures force the water up to the surface without any need for a pump. They are called artesian wells because some of the earliest such wells were drilled in the 1700s near Artois, in France.

There is also substantial oil and gas production in Dimmit County.

Carrizo Springs has been the county seat of Dimmit County since the county was organized. The present courthouse was built in 1926.

Dimmit County does not quite touch the border, so there is no border crossing here, and no freeway comes through the county. But U.S. 83 and U.S. 277 meet at Carrizo Springs.

Quail and doves, deer and javelinas are plentiful here. Hunters can make their own arrangements with landowners or apply to the State Department of Parks and Wildlife for permits to hunt in the Chaparral Wildlife Management Area on Farm Road 133 at the eastern edge of the county.

N

Del Rio and the Middle Border

Maverick, Zavala, Kinney, Uvalde, Real,
Edwards, Sutton, Crockett, Val Verde
counties.

We encourage you to begin your tour of this part of the state at Eagle Pass and then swing up through the Edwards plateau country and back south to Del Rio, Amistad and Langtry. Del Rio or Uvalde would be suitable bases if you prefer to stop in one place and make side trips.

Travelers new to the west will begin to see some unfamiliar plants in this part of the state. There are hundreds of varieties of cactus and various other desert plants growing from here on westward. The cactus garden at the Roy Bean Visitors' Center the Texas Department of Highways and Public Transportation maintains at Langtry is a good place to find out something about these desert plants. (See page 241.)

The early inhabitants of this part of Texas left hundreds of pictures and symbols on the rock walls of the river canyons and caves here. Some of these rock paintings are accessible and there are some references to specific locations in the section on Val Verde County. If you would like to know more about these haunting examples of primitive art, we recommend a book published by the University of Texas Press in 1967 called *Rock Art of Texas Indians* by Forrest Kirkland and W. W. Newcomb Jr.

MAVERICK COUNTY
Texas ranchers refer to range animals without any brand as mavericks. The term has been in use since about 1845 when

The word maverick is so much a part of our language now that it is in Webster's Dictionary. The word is generally defined as meaning an unbranded calf but it is also used sometimes to describe a person of independent mind. The Maverick family of Texas contributed this word to the language unintentionally. It started when Sam Maverick neglected to brand some calves, in the 1840s. Sam was one of the signers of the Declaration of Independence. It was for that, more than for failing to brand his calves, that the legislature named this border county for Sam Maverick.

early settler Samuel Augustus Maverick received some cattle from one of his creditors in payment of a debt. Maverick's employee in charge of the cows neglected to put a brand on them, and other ranchers recognized the cows as Maverick's because they had no brands. The name stuck, and all unbranded cows came to be called mavericks.

Samuel Maverick also gave his name to this county. He was one of the leaders of the Texas revolution and one of the most distinguished citizens of the Republic of Texas, and he was still living when the legislature created this county from part of Kinney County and named it for him in 1856.

Samuel Maverick came to Texas from Alabama in 1835 and immediately joined the revolutionary army. He was a member of the Texas force that captured the Alamo in 1835. He was a delegate to the convention of 1836, and he was one of the signers of the Declaration of Independence. Maverick went back to Alabama to get married and missed the war that followed the declaration of 1836. He returned to Texas in 1838, and he served as mayor of San Antonio, as a member of the congress of the Republic, and as a member of the state legislature. Maverick died in San Antonio in 1870. His grandson, Maury Maverick, was mayor of San Antonio from 1936 until 1938.

The principal town in Maverick County began as a border military post before the county was created. That post became Eagle Pass. It is the county seat. The original courthouse was built in 1884. It is still in use. There is some oil and gas production here, but agriculture is a bigger factor in the economy. Some irrigated farms along the Rio Grande

Eagle Pass is the principal town and the county seat of Maverick County. The name was borrowed from a place on the other side of the Rio Grande. The county was established in 1856. The present courthouse was built in 1884 and it is still in use. This may be the only courthouse in Texas with a clock that is still wound by hand. There aren't as many courthouse clocks as there used to be and most of those remaining have been electrified.

here produce three crops per year.

The old Spanish road from Mexico to Nacogdoches crossed the Rio Grande about thirty miles south of Eagle Pass in what is now Maverick County, so some of the earliest travelers came through here.

Eagle Pass started as a Texas militia camp. A smugglers' trail crossed the Rio Grande here near the junction of the Rio Grande and the Rio Escondido. The militia outpost was established near the crossing by a volunteer company commanded by Captain John Veatch in 1848. Veatch borrowed the name of a crossing on the Escondido on the Mexican side of the border and called his post Eagle Pass.

The U.S. Army established a post in the area the following year and called it Fort Duncan. The fort was established to protect the border and to protect the covered wagon caravans traveling to the California goldfields. The town of Eagle Pass grew up around the fort. The first commercial establishment, naturally, was a saloon. It was started by a dropout from one of the California wagon trains. His name was Henry Matson. He established his business with two kegs of whiskey he bought from the wagon train and a tent he borrowed from one of the soldiers at Fort Duncan. The first settlers were

The city of Eagle Pass began as a border military post and the border post eventually became a full-fledged fort. The army transferred old Fort Duncan to the city in 1938 and the property overlooking the Rio Grande is now a city park and golf course. The old fort headquarters building is now a museum.

discharged soldiers and dropouts from other wagon trains. There was a stage line to San Antonio by 1851, but this area was infested with bandits and gunmen until the Civil War began in 1861. Eagle Pass was an important trading center for the Confederacy during the Civil War. Southern cotton passing through here to the world markets earned money to help sustain the Southern cause.

Eagle Pass also figured in an incident that might be labeled the last gasp of the Confederacy. General Joseph Orville Shelby was the commander of the Missouri Raiders stationed in Texas at the time General Lee surrendered to General Grant at Appomattox. Shelby refused to abide by the surrender agreement. He marched his troops to Del Rio and crossed the Rio Grande to avoid giving in to the Union forces. Shelby wrapped his Confederate flag and the plume from his hat around a rock and sank them in the middle of the Rio Grande. The general offered his troops a choice when they reached Mexico. They could offer their services to the emperor Maximilian or to his opponent, Benito Juárez. The Confederate veterans predictably voted for Maximilian. But the emperor declined their offer. It was one of his mistakes. The refugees were offered land, and some of them settled in Mexico. General Shelby stayed there until 1868. But then he returned to Missouri. A state historical marker at 100 Garrison Street in Eagle Pass commemorates the burial of the Shelby flag.

United States troops returned to Fort Duncan after the Civil War. Ranchers moved into the area, and the railroad

The international toll bridge connects the downtown section of Eagle Pass directly with the plaza in Piedras Negras, Mexico. Travelers can park their cars in Eagle Pass and walk across the bridge and the most promising shop on the Mexican side is right at the bridge. This is one of the Centros Artesanals the Mexican government operates. Offered for sale are the best examples of authentic Mexican folk art, jewelry, furniture, textiles and ceramic work.

reached Eagle Pass in 1882. Several coal mines were developed to supply coal to the locomotives. There is coal on both sides of the border here. It crops out of the ground so conspicuously that it provided the name for the Mexican town across the river from Eagle Pass. Piedras Negras is Spanish for black rocks, and the black rocks are coal. The demand for coal declined when the locomotives on the Texas side of the border began burning oil, and it ended when the locomotives on the Mexican side of the border started burning oil about the time of World War II.

Old Fort Duncan was taken over by the city of Eagle Pass in 1938, and it is now a city park and country club.

The Seminole Negro Scouts were organized here after the Civil War to put an end to the Indian problem on this section of the frontier. Their contribution and other historical events are depicted in exhibits in the Fort Duncan Museum in Fort Duncan Park. There is a small admission fee. The museum is open daily except Sundays in the summer, and only on weekends the rest of the year.

Nearly a dozen of the original Fort Duncan buildings are preserved here. Many famous soldiers were stationed here, including Philip Sheridan, John Bullis, Jimmy Doolittle and Matthew Ridgway. One of the big events in the early history of aviation was recorded here in 1911 when a Wright Scout

There are some elegant old homes on Ceylon Street in Eagle Pass. Ceylon Street is Highway 277. These are all private residences and not open to the public.

biplane landed safely on the Fort Duncan parade ground after a flight from Laredo. It was the first time anybody had flown 106 miles, non-stop.

Some fine old homes built right after the turn of the century line Ceylon Street in Eagle Pass, and several original stone and adobe homes are still standing north of Main Street in the downtown section.

A fairly new international bridge links Eagle Pass with Piedras Negras on the Mexican side of the Rio Grande, and there is a highway from Piedras Negras on into Saltillo, San Luis Potosi and Mexico City. This is Mexican Highway 57. It passes by the city that once was the capital of the Mexican state of Coahuila and Texas. The former capital is Monclova, approximately 150 miles south of Piedras Negras. The building that was the capitol was an adobe hall built in 1689. It was torn down in 1967. The Monclova City Hall now stands on the site, on the central plaza. There is a small plaque on the building recalling that the capitol of Coahuila and Texas once stood here. You will need a tourist card, proof that you own the vehicle you are driving and Mexican auto insurance if you are going beyond Piedras Negras.

ZAVALA COUNTY
There are 254 counties in Texas. In the alphabetical list,

Some of the heroes of the Texas revolution were Mexicans. Lorenzo de Zavala was one of them. He was born in Mexico while it was still Spanish. He held office during the Spanish rule and in the Mexican government after Mexico gained independence. De Zavala became disenchanted with President Santa Anna in 1835 and joined the revolutionary movement in Texas. He was a signer of the Declaration of Independence and he was named vice-president of the interim government that managed the revolution, to the extent that it was managed. Santa Anna considered de Zavala the worst traitor in the Texas camp. The Texas legislature expressed its different view in naming this county for de Zavala when it was created in 1858.

Zavala ranks 254th. Zavala County was created in 1858 from parts of Maverick and Uvalde counties. But the county was not actually organized until 1884. The original county seat was Batesville because it was about the only town in the county at the time.

Some of the earliest travelers came through here because this area was on the main route from Eagle Pass to San Antonio and the Spanish missions in the east. Nobody settled here until the late 1860s and early 1870s. The first settler probably was Mont Woodward. He established a ranch on the Leona River and very shortly after that, the Bates family settled nearby. Their settlement became Batesville. The Bates brothers probably were the first to use irrigation in farming here. Their place was known as Bates' Ditch until it became the county seat and needed a more dignified name.

The county seat was moved to Crystal City in 1928. The present courthouse was built in 1963. Crystal City was founded in 1907 by E. J. Buckingham and Carl Groos. They apparently had the good luck to know that the site was going to be on the first railroad to be built through the county. They subdivided what had been the Cross S Ranch and sold off lots. The railroad came through in 1908. Crystal City has been the principal shipping point ever since. The land here was devoted mostly to ranching before that time. The arrival of the railroad and the drilling of artesian wells turned a number of ranches into truck farms. Farm crops now produce about as much income as livestock in Zavala County. The principal crops are cotton and vegetables, especially onions

1

1) *The county seat for Zavala County was not established at Crystal City until 1928. The town of Batesville had been the seat of the government before that. The courthouse at Crystal City is not your everyday Texas courthouse. It is a glass box, built in 1963. 2) Many Texas cities claim to be the capital of something or other. Crystal City advertises itself as the spinach capital. This is the reason there is a statue of Popeye outside the city hall here. Popeye did more for spinach in comics and cartoons than Del Monte and Bird's Eye together have done.*

2

and spinach. Crystal City claims to be the spinach capital, and there has been a statue of Popeye standing on the square in downtown Crystal City since 1937. There are several vegetable packing plants here, and the county has some oil and gas production.

There was an alien detention camp for Japanese here during World War II. Some of the old buildings are now being used by the Crystal City School System.

Zavala County was named for Lorenzo de Zavala. The name was misspelled in the original act of the legislature that created the county, and for a time the name of the county was spelled with two *l's:* Zavalla. The spelling has since been corrected. Lorenzo de Zavala was born in Mexico in 1789, while Mexico and Texas were still Spanish territory. He had the distinction of holding office in the Spanish government and in the Mexican government and in the interim government of the Republic of Texas. De Zavala was representing Yucatan in the Spanish Parliament when Mexico declared its independence. He served in Parliament, and he was secretary of

1) Crystal City is another case where the artesian wells the railroads discovered led to irrigated farming. Ditch irrigation and sprinklers coax rich crops out of the level land around here. 2) One of the less noble acts committed by our government during World War II was the detention of Japanese-Americans in camps we would have called concentration camps if somebody else had built them. One of the camps was outside Crystal City. Some of the buildings are falling in. One of them is being used as a school. There has been talk among some Japanese-Americans of trying to preserve some of this camp as a kind of memorial to the people who were confined here.

the treasury, and he was governor of the state of Mexico in the early days of Mexican independence. De Zavala was serving as Mexico's minister to France when he decided in 1835 that Santa Anna was betraying the Mexican Constitution of 1824. He gave up his office and his allegiance to Santa Anna's regime. He moved to Texas and joined the movement for separation from Mexico. De Zavala was a delegate to the convention of 1836 at Washington-on-the-Brazos. He signed the Declaration of Independence there, and he was elected vice-president of the interim government. He died just a few months after his side won the battle at San Jacinto. Santa Anna always thought de Zavala's changing sides was one of the most outrageous things that happened in the Texas Revolution.

The old road from Eagle Pass to San Antonio crossed the Nueces River north of the present town of La Pryor. The Frontier Regiment established an outpost at this crossing during the Civil War. It was called Camp Nueces, and there is a marker at the site in a roadside park on U.S. 83, eight miles

The man this county was named for was one of the busiest men on the Texas frontier. Henry L. Kinney came to Texas from Pennsylvania in 1838. He became a rancher and trader. He and his partners had a fleet of ships in the Gulf and fleets of freight wagons in Texas. Kinney helped to found the city of Corpus Christi, and he served in the Congress of the Republic and in the legislature after Texas became a state. He moved to Mexico during the Civil War because he was not in sympathy with the Confederate cause and he was killed in Mexico in some kind of dispute in the 1860s.

north of La Pryor. The Frontier Regiment was formed in 1861 to take over the job the U.S. Army had previously done guarding the Texas frontier against the Indians and outlaws.

KINNEY COUNTY

Kinney County was created by the legislature in 1850, but it was not organized until 1874. The county was named for colonial trader Henry Lawrence Kinney. He was the founder of the city of Corpus Christi.

The county seat is the town of Brackettville. The town grew up around an army post established in 1852. Fort Clark was named, as most of the Texas border forts were, for an American soldier killed in the war with Mexico. This fort was named for Major John B. Clark. It was established to protect travelers and settlers from the Indians.

A stage line from San Antonio to El Paso passed through here. The Seminole Negro Scouts were based here. These scouts were men descended from Negro slaves and Seminole Indians. They were especially good at tracking Indian war parties and there is a tribute to them on a state historical marker in the Seminole Scout Cemetery, five miles south of Brackettville on a local road that branches off U.S. 90.

Fort Clark was an important army post from the time it was established until it was sold off to private interests in 1946. It was established by units of the First Infantry and units of the Second, Third, Fourth and Fifth Cavalry were stationed here at later times. Texas volunteers occupied the

1) The stage line between San Antonio and El Paso came through Brackettville. And this old building was the stage stop. It has not had much attention recently. 2) Brackettville is not a ghost town. It is growing. But there are many antique and abandoned buildings in the older sections of the city. The Filipone family came here in the early days and built this building that probably would have been right at home in the Filipone's native Italy. The family operated a store on the ground floor and lived on the second floor.

fort during the Civil War and the U.S. Army re-occupied it in 1866. There was substantial new construction at the fort in the 1860s and 1870s, but the government did not have title to the land and did not acquire title until 1884, when the army paid Samuel Maverick's widow 80,000 dollars for the site the troops had been occupying since 1852. The old buildings are stone, and they are in good condition. The fort was a private resort and conference center for several years, and it is now a club. Famous soldiers served here. Jonathan Wainwright built the big swimming pool here, in defiance of army red tape. John L. Bullis was stationed here with the Seminole Scouts. He received a special commendation from the Texas legislature for his efforts to protect the frontier. Ulysses Grant and Robert E. Lee also were stationed here at various times.

A Spanish expedition checking on Robert La Salle's landing in Texas made a strange discovery near the present site of Brackettville in 1688. It is recorded on a state historical marker on U.S. Highway 90 near the State Highway Depart-

1) *This old house has deteriorated to the point that it makes a good illustration of the type of construction the Mexicans call palisado. The building begins with poles driven into the ground, vertically. Smaller sticks are laid on horizontally. The openings are filled with mud and rocks and then plastered over.* 2) *The county government conducts its business now in this building, built in 1910.* 3) *But the original Kinney County Courthouse is still standing on the same grounds with the newer one. The Brackettville Post Office is on the ground floor. The Masonic Lodge occupies the second floor.*

2

3

ment's warehouse that the Spanish found a Frenchman named Jean Henri living here like a king with a tribe of Indians. Henri apparently was a stray member of the La Salle expedition that landed on the Texas coast by mistake while looking for the mouth of the Mississippi. What the Spanish explorer Alonso de León was able to learn from Henri helped him to find the site of La Salle's Fort St. Louis on Matagorda Bay in 1689. By that time La Salle had been murdered and his followers had scattered. The French had made no actual attempt to settle or claim Texas, but their blunder caused the Spanish to reinforce their claim by establishing roads and missions across Texas.

The present courthouse in Brackettville was built in 1910. The original courthouse, built about 1879, is still standing, too, on the courthouse square. The older building now houses

1) This old commissary building at Fort Clark is standing empty, but many of the buildings have been converted into homes and condominiums and Fort Clark is now a private residential community. 2) The oldest building at Fort Clark is called the Robert E. Lee Courthouse. Lee is said to have conducted some courts martial in this building when he was stationed on the Texas frontier before the Civil War. 3) This is called the Wainwright house because Lt. General Jonathan Wainwright was stationed here just before he was sent to the Philippines. Wainwright was left to surrender the U.S. troops at Corregidor when Douglas MacArthur went to Australia. Wainwright had little choice and he was generally regarded as a hero. He was a hero at Fort Clark, too. He wanted to build a swimming pool at the Las Moras spring on the base. The army never got around to approving the idea, but Wainwright found a way to build it anyway. 4) The pool is as big as a football field with cold spring water circulating through it.

1

1) *Ruins of the original headquarters building at Fort Clark. The post was named for one of the casualties of the war with Mexico, Major John B. Clark. 2) The Seminole Indian Scouts were part Indian and part Negro. Their specialty was tracking hostile Indian parties and they apparently were extraordinary soldiers. 3) John L. Bullis was appointed a major general just before he retired from the U.S. Army in 1905. He was cited especially for his work with the Seminole Indian Scouts against the Comanches in this area.*

2

3

the Brackettville post office and Masonic Lodge. The St. Mary Magdalene Catholic Church at El Paso and Keene streets dates from 1878.

The principal tourist attraction in Kinney County is the Alamo Village on the Shahan Angus Ranch six miles north of Brackettville on Ranch Road 674. This is where John Wayne made his movie *The Alamo.* The replica of the Alamo had to be partially destroyed during the filming, of course. It is still in ruins, but the replica of the village of San Antonio is in good shape, and it comes to life every summer. The cantina serves refreshments. Stagecoaches come and go, and employees periodically fire blank cartridges at each other for the entertainment of the visitors. There is a charge for admission to the Alamo Village.

1) There is another Alamo more suited to visitors with rambunctious children than the one at San Antonio is. This one was built for the John Wayne movie about the battle. Visitors to Alamo Village can wander and climb around the ruins freely. 2) Some of the buildings are shops, now. And there is a stagecoach that takes visitors riding around the grounds. 3) Entertainment here includes mock gunfights on the main street.

1

1) *Ranching is the biggest enterprise in Uvalde County. Many of the ranches raise cattle, but this is sheep and goat country, too. Former Governor Dolph Briscoe is one of the big ranchers here.*
2) *The city of Uvalde was founded by a rancher named Reading W. Black. He established the first store here in the 1850s. Black was not able to work up much enthusiasm for the Confederate cause during the Civil War and that may have been what caused a relative to shoot him to death in 1867.*

2

UVALDE COUNTY

Uvalde County is the home of former Governor Dolph Briscoe. He has been described as the biggest landowner in Texas, and much of the land he owns is in this county. Briscoe is a rancher. Ranching is the biggest business in Uvalde County. Cattle, sheep and goats produce most of the income here, but there is some gas production and tourists generate a lot of business.

The first Europeans here were Spanish soldiers and missionaries. They established the Mission Nuestra Senora de la Candelaria del Canon on the Nueces near the present town of Montell in 1762. The purpose was to convert the Apaches and give them some protection from the Comanches. The effort did not succeed. The mission was abandoned after a few years, and the Comanches continued to have things their way. Comanche raids kept Spanish settlements on the Rio Grande in a state of anxiety, and a Spanish officer named Juan de Ugalde led several forays into this area to punish the raiders.

1) Uvalde County was organized in 1856 and the present courthouse at Uvalde was built in 1927. A granite marker on the courthouse grounds recalls that there was an army camp named Fort Inge here from 1849 to 1869. 2) The first Texan to be elected to high national office was John Nance Garner. He was elected county judge here and then was elected to Congress in 1903. Garner became vice-president in 1932.

He won some skirmishes with the Indians. So when it came time to pick a name for this county, somebody suggested Captain Juan's name, and it was picked. Uvalde is a misspelling of Ugalde's name. The Comanches continued to harass settlers after Texas separated from Mexico and joined the United States. The U.S. Army established a post here in 1849. It was called Fort Inge. The Confederates took it over in 1861. Fort Inge was re-occupied by U.S. troops in 1866 and then abandoned in 1869. The old fort was four and a half miles southeast of the present city of Uvalde. There is a state marker at the site.

Uvalde County was organized in 1856 from part of the original Bexar County. The county seat is the city of Uvalde. The city grew from a settlement originally named Encina. The settlement was founded by Reading W. Black in 1853. Black and a partner established a ranch first and then Black built a store and started a couple of rock quarries and laid out a townsite. The name of the settlement was changed when the county was organized, and the settlement was chosen to be the county seat. The present courthouse was built in 1927.

Founder Black became a fairly unpopular man here before he died. He objected to the way Texas Confederates treated German settlers loyal to the Union cause during the Civil War. Black moved to Mexico until the war was over. He

1

1) Garner returned to Uvalde in 1941 and lived here until he died in 1967. Mrs. Garner died in 1948 and Garner gave the family home to the city of Uvalde in her memory. He lived the remainder of his life in a small cottage behind the main house, shelling pecans and conversing with a steady stream of visitors. The home is now a museum. 2) J. K. "King" Fisher was a deputy and running unopposed for election to sheriff in 1884 when he was ambushed and killed in a theater in San Antonio. Fisher had been an officer of the law earlier, chasing cattle rustlers. But it was said that he changed sides and led the rustlers for a while. He was blamed for eleven murders, but he was never convicted.

2

returned after the war and became active in Unionist politics. His political career did not last long. He was shot to death in 1867. Some of Black's accomplishments are recorded on a state marker at Main and East streets in Uvalde.

The late John Nance Garner made his home in Uvalde. Garner was vice-president during Franklin D. Roosevelt's first two terms. Garner died here, and he is buried here, in the Uvalde Cemetery on U.S. 90 on the west side of town. Garner's old home in the 300 block of North Park Street is now a museum. It is open every day except Sunday, and there is no admission fee. The Garner estate has recently given the city the old Uvalde Opera House, and it is due to be restored.

Pat Garrett lived in Uvalde for a while. The house is no longer standing, but there is a marker where it stood, on the grounds of the State Highway Department Headquarters on U.S. 90. Garrett became a frontier legend when he killed

1) Uvalde had one of the theaters that was fairly standard for Texas towns in the late 1800s and early 1900s. It was an auditorium above a store and it was called the Opera House in Uvalde, as in a hundred other Texas county seats. The Opera House is one of the Uvalde buildings displaying a state historical marker. 2) Another one is the old Bertha Dalton home which is a private residence. 3) An old hotel in downtown Uvalde has been restored and turned into a combination office building and apartment house. This building was known as the Rice Hotel and as the Courtyard Hotel at various times earlier.

badman Billy the Kid Bonney at Fort Sumner, New Mexico, in 1881. Garrett was sheriff of Lincoln County, New Mexico, at the time. It was some time after that that Garrett moved to Uvalde. He did not stay here long. He was back in New Mexico wearing a sheriff's badge again by 1896. He was shot to death in a dispute with another man there in 1908.

Uvalde County had a more colorful character of its own in J. K. "King" Fisher. Fisher operated on both sides of the law at various times. He was suspected of rustling cattle, and he was blamed for eleven murders. He was chasing rustlers as a lawman at other times. He wore dashing Mexican costumes and silver-plated revolvers, and he was running for sheriff of Uvalde County when he was ambushed and killed in a theater in San Antonio in 1884. King Fisher is buried in the Pioneer Cemetery in Uvalde.

Uvalde buildings with state historical markers include:

● The Opera House at East North Street and Getty.

1

1) A newer landmark in downtown Uvalde is Dolph Briscoe's First State Bank. Mrs. Briscoe has furnished it with rare antiques and western art. 2) The Slade Saddle Shop in Uvalde has been making boots and saddles and other leather products by hand since 1883. 3) This is the only state park we know of with a song named for it. Garner State Park is very popular with campers, especially. It is on the Frio River, north of Uvalde on U.S. Highway 83.

2

3

These markers remind us that the Spanish had a mission here at Montell in the 1760s. The mission was part of the unsuccessful effort to make Christians of the Apaches and protect them from the Comanches. There is not much here except the markers, but the trip to see them is worth it because Texas Highway 55, between Uvalde and Rocksprings, is as pretty a drive as you can find.

● The Bertha Dalton house at 543 North Getty.

Dolph Briscoe's First State Bank is one of the sights to see in downtown Uvalde. It is furnished with Victorian antiques.

The old Courtyard Hotel, built about 1900, has been restored as a combination office building and apartment house. The Courtyard is on North East Street, across from the courthouse.

The Slade Saddle Shop at 112 North East Street was founded in 1883, and it is still turning out leather goods made by hand.

One of the most popular state parks in Texas is north of Uvalde on scenic U.S. Highway 83. Garner State Park on the Frio River is one of the state's Class I parks. There is an entrance fee of two dollars per vehicle unless you have an annual pass. There are additional charges for the use of cabins, shelters or campsites. Garner Park has eighteen cabins for rent, forty screened shelters, and 143 campsites. The address for reservations is Garner State Park, Concan, Texas 78838. The phone number is 512-232-6633. The annual passes for Texas State Parks are now fifteen dollars. People over the age of sixty-five can enter state parks free if they obtain the state Parklands Passport. The State Department of Parks and Wildlife will send you a leaflet with more details on state

1) The Spanish interest in the Lipan Apaches led to the establishment of another mission in the Nueces valley just a few miles north of the one at the present site of Montell, in Real County. The Mission San Lorenzo de la Santa Cruz operated three tenths of a mile north of the present town of Camp Wood from about 1762 to 1768. 2) The markers for the Mission San Lorenzo and Camp Wood are only a few feet apart. But the actual site of the original Camp Wood is about one fifth of a mile north of here. Charles Lindbergh crashed a plane into a hardware store near here in 1924.

parks if you write to the department at 4200 Smith School Road, Austin, Texas 78744.

A state marker at Silver Mine Pass, south of Concan, reminds us there was once a silver mine here. It was not a big one. Most of the silver mines in Texas were west of the Pecos. But the mine here did produce some silver in the 1830s. The marker is in the roadside park where U.S. 83 and State Highway 127 meet.

Reagan Wells, west of Garner State Park, is one of those towns where the discovery of mineral wells created a little resort. It flourished for a few years in the early 1900s.

Montell, in the canyon of the Nueces, on State Highway 55, in the northwest corner of Uvalde County, was the site of the Mission Nuestra Senora de la Candelaria del Canon. There is a marker at the site, off Highway 55.

REAL COUNTY

The first settlement in what is now Real County was a Spanish mission. The Mission San Lorenzo de la Santa Cruz was established on the Nueces River here in 1762 to make Christians out of the Lipan Apaches. The mission was not a big success, and the Spanish abandoned it about 1768. The United States Army established an outpost here in 1857 to protect settlers and travelers from the Indians. The post was named Camp Wood in honor of the lieutenant commanding

1

2

1) Several rivers rise from springs in this part of the Edwards plateau. The Frio rises in northern Real County. Farm Road 336, paralleling the Frio north of Leakey is one of several very scenic drives in this county. 2) The little town of Leakey has been the county seat for two different counties. It was the county seat for Edwards County when all of this area was Edwards County. It became the county seat for Real County when Real was split off from Edwards, Kerr and Bandera counties. That was in 1913. The present courthouse was built in 1918. There is a new addition designed to blend with the original limestone building.

the troops initially stationed here. Materials from the old Spanish mission were used in the building of Camp Wood. But the camp did not last long, either. The troops surrendered to the Texas Confederates at the beginning of the Civil War in 1861, and the camp never was active after that. But the Apaches and Comanches continued to make occasional raids on settlements here until 1879.

The present town of Camp Wood is approximately on the site of the old army outpost. The ruins of the original Spanish mission were excavated in 1962. They are accessible, and they are listed in the *National Register of Historic Places,* and marked with Texas historical markers. The mission site is three tenths of a mile north of Camp Wood, on State Highway 55. The Camp Wood site is five tenths of a mile

1

1) The Prade Ranch on the Frio River and Farm Road 336 north of Leakey was one of the early centers of dude ranching. Dude ranching does not turn on as many people as it once did, and the Prade Ranch now operates as a private working ranch. 2) Goats thrive on the sparse vegetation that grows between the rocks here in Real County. Ranching is the principal occupation here and Real County is a leader in the production of mohair. Mohair is the hair of the Angora goat.

north of town, on State Highway 55.

Real County was created in 1913 from parts of Bandera, Edwards and Kerr counties. It was named for Julius Real. He was a member of the Texas House of Representatives and later a member of the state senate. Real was born on a ranch near Kerrville in 1860, and he died in 1944, at the age of eighty-four, in the same house he was born in. His name and the name of the county are pronounced re-*al.*

The county seat is Leakey. The present courthouse was built in 1918, and an addition built in 1979 was designed to blend with it. There is no *leak* in Leakey. The name is pronounced *lay*-ky. The town was named for John L. Leakey. He was the first settler here. Leakey built a cabin in the Frio River canyon in 1857, while the area was still part of Bandera County. A little settlement developed. Part of the settlement was included in Edwards County when Edwards

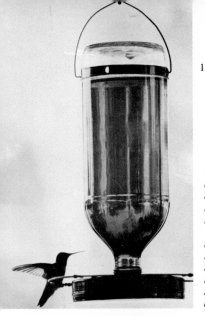

1) Hummingbirds enjoy sugared water and they find it more readily if it is dyed red. So householders and ranchers all over this part of the state hang out containers of red sugared water for the hummingbirds. 2) Hummingbird feeders hang all around the Frio Canyon Lodge at Leakey so the busy little birds flock here in substantial numbers. Some visitors choose the Frio Canyon Lodge because of the hummingbirds.

County was formed in 1883, and Leakey became the county seat of Edwards County. The people of Edwards County voted to move their county seat to Rocksprings in 1891. But Leakey became a county seat again when it became part of Real County.

Leakey has been the county seat for two counties, and it is well over one hundred years old, but it has not grown much. The population is under five hundred. There is no industry here. There is no mineral production of any consequence, but there were a couple of kaolin mines in the earlier days along Camp Wood Creek between Leakey and Camp Wood. Kaolin is a fine white clay used in making porcelain and paper

Beer commercials speak of a country of eleven hundred springs. The count may not be exact, but this is the part of the country that phrase refers to and there is one cliff here in the northwest corner of Edwards County that is called Seven Hundred Springs. Cold water rushes out of countless crannies in the limestone. This is where the South Llano River begins. The springs are on private property.

coatings.

This is the Edwards plateau. There is some spectacular scenery here with modest mountains rising to around 2,400 feet, and the Nueces and Frio rivers. Especially scenic is U.S. 83 northeast out of Leakey. You can go north on U.S. 83 until you reach Texas 41, turn left and continue west until you reach Farm Road 336. Turn left again and travel south along the Frio River, back to Leakey. Farm Road 337 from Leakey to Camp Wood is another pleasant drive.

Real County is part of the Texas goat country. There are some cattle and sheep ranches, too. The Prade Ranch on the Frio River north of Leakey was a popular dude resort for a number of years, beginning in the middle 1930s. It was such a fixture that it shows up on some maps as a town. But it is not a town and it is not accommodating dudes anymore, either. It is a private ranch.

Some people visit Leakey in the summer, especially to see the hummingbirds. Mr. and Mrs. Johnny Pope run the restaurant at the Frio Canyon Lodge. They keep their bird feeders filled with sugared water stained with a red dye. And the hummingbirds flock here in the summer like the swallows flock to Capistrano.

EDWARDS COUNTY

There really is a land of eleven hundred springs. It is not just a commercial for beer. There is such a place, and this is the place. This is the Edwards plateau.

1

2

1) The town of Rocksprings was established in 1891 because of the presence here of a natural spring. The site is a city park, now, but the rock spring has dried up. One theory is that the water was diverted when the settlers began to drill wells in the area. 2) Rocksprings still has its original courthouse, built in 1891. The building was almost destroyed by fire in 1898 and damaged by a tornado in 1927. But it was repaired and looks sturdy enough to stand for another hundred years.

There is one place in the northwestern tip of this county called Seven Hundred Springs. Floods have destroyed some of the original beauty of this spot, but there are cold springs here, still, and in many other parts of Edwards County, too. The South Llano River and the east and west forks of the Nueces River all rise within the boundaries of Edwards County. They say that the water that falls on the courthouse square in Rocksprings runs off into four different streams.

Edwards County was created in 1858 from part of the original Bexar district. It was not organized formally until 1883. The county was named for Haden Edwards. He was one of the early settlers in the Nacogdoches area. He probably never set foot in this county, but he did make several trips between Nacogdoches and Matamoros, trading in cattle and mules. Edwards rose from captain to brigadier general in the Texas army. He served in the Congress of the Republic, and he served in the legislature after Texas joined the Union.

Leakey was the original county seat of Edwards County. Leakey became the county seat of Real County when it was

1

2

1) The original county jail is still standing at Rocksprings, too. It is not used much. They don't have much occasion to lock people up here. It is a sort of unofficial public comfort station. The restrooms on the ground floor are open and available to passersby, a more civilized arrangement than you'll find in most towns. 2) The Guide to Official Texas Historical Markers published by the Texas Historical Commission says there is a marker on the old Carson Building in Rocksprings. But the operators of Sorrell's Grocery and Market now occupying the building say they don't know anything about a marker. The building was one of the few in Rocksprings to survive the twister of 1927 that killed 27 people.

formed from parts of Edwards, Bandera and Kerr counties, and Rocksprings became the county seat of Edwards County in 1891. The courthouse was built in Rocksprings that same year. It burned in 1898, and most of the early county records were lost in that fire. But the old courthouse was rebuilt after the fire and it is still in use.

There is some oil and gas production here, but ranching is still the principal activity. Angora goats, sheep and cattle are the biggest factors in the economy of Edwards County, but tourism and hunting are important, too.

Goats of several varieties are found on the ranches in Edwards County. These are Spanish goats, hardly as aristocratic as the shaggier animals that have inspired Edwards County to nominate itself the Angora Capital of the World. But this one knows how to shake hands.

The oldest community in the county is Barksdale. The first settler was L. M. Pullen. He settled on a grant on Cedar Creek in 1876. He called his settlement Dixie, but it was renamed Barksdale, after Louis Barksdale moved here in 1880.

Some of the early settlers experimented with growing cotton here, and there was a cotton gin in Barksdale in 1887. There are markers in Barksdale commemorating the massacre of Nick Coalson's family in 1879, the original Dixie settlement, and the old Nix Mill, all on State Highway 55, in Barksdale.

Rocksprings was not laid out by J. R. Sweeten until 1890. It never had a boom. The population is not yet fifteen hundred. This is one county where the railroads did not dictate which towns would and would not survive. The first railroad has yet to reach Edwards County.

Some of the buildings bearing historical markers in Rocksprings are the courthouse, the Carson Building at Well and Austin streets, the Hough Haven house on Sweeten two blocks north of the square, and the old Rocksprings school site at State Highway 55 and U.S. 377.

The scenery along U.S. 377 in both directions out of Rocksprings is worth seeing.

SUTTON COUNTY
Sutton County is part of the Edwards plateau. This is ranch

1) The first settlement in what is now Sutton County was one of the U.S. Army's frontier forts. Fort Terrett was established on the North Llano River here in 1852. The fort was abandoned a few years later, but a couple of the old buildings have been restored and turned into private homes. 2) The marker at the site of Fort Terrett is thirty miles east of Sonora and two miles north of the highway, on the River Road. The houses here are not open to the public.

country. There is also substantial oil and gas production here.

Sutton County was created by the legislature from part of Crockett County in 1887. It was organized in 1890. The county was named for John S. Sutton. He came to Texas from Delaware in 1840. He missed the revolution, but he fought with the Texas army in various skirmishes with the Mexicans and the Indians. He was a lieutenant colonel with the Seventh Texas Cavalry in the Confederate army when he was killed in 1862.

The first Anglo settlement here was Fort Terrett on the north Llano River. It was established in 1852 as part of the chain of forts the U.S. Army built to protect settlers and travelers from the Indians after Texas joined the Union. Fort Terrett was abandoned in 1854, probably because the army was establishing Fort Lancaster, a little farther west about that time. Fort Terrett and Fort Lancaster both were on the

1) *The old Santa Fe Passenger Depot at Sonora is closed and nailed up, like many others. But this one is nowhere near as old as some of the other abandoned stations are. 2) Sonora waited a long time for railroad service. So a substantial crowd turned out when the depot was new to await the arrival of the first train. That was 1930. Ranchers here had to walk their cows one hundred miles to the railroad at Brady before that.*

1

2

old road from San Antonio to El Paso. What is left of Fort Lancaster is in Crockett County, west of here. The site of Fort Terrett is marked with one of the state's historical markers. It is thirty miles east of Sonora, two miles north of U.S. 290 on the River Road.

The town of Sonora has been the county seat of Sutton County since the county was organized. The present courthouse was built in 1891. It is the original courthouse. Settlement of Sonora began before the county was formed. The first settler was a sheep rancher named E. M. Kirkland. He came in 1879. The town had more than seven hundred people by 1900. The first railroad did not reach Sonora until 1930. There was a fenced cattle trail between here and Brady before that. Ranchers drove their cattle to the railroad at Brady along this trail. It was 250 feet wide and a hundred miles long. And there was a stage line operating here until 1915, carrying passengers and mail between Sonora and San Angelo. Old bones found in Devil's Draw here indicate that humans lived where Sutton County is now thousands of years

1) *The first settler came here in 1879. Sutton County was created in 1887. The first courthouse was built in Sonora in 1891 and it is still in use. The county was named for a Confederate colonel. 2) The Miers Museum in Sonora has a collection of furnishings and implements and photographs from pioneer days, housed in the old Miers ranch house. It is usually open only on Tuesday afternoons. 3) A marker outside the old Sutton County Jail recalls that the first prisoner locked up here was a cousin of the notorious gunman John Wesley Hardin. The jail was built in 1891.*

1

2

3

ago.

Some of the finest wool and mohair in the country comes from here, and it passes through the Sonora Wool and Mohair Company on its way to the big woolen mills.

The Miers Museum at 309 Oak Street is housed in one of the oldest homes in Sonora. Ike Miers came here by covered wagon, and he built this house as headquarters for his ranch in 1888. Displays in the museum trace some of the area's history. There is no charge for admission, but the museum was open only on Tuesday afternoons at the last report. The old courthouse and the old jail are other places of special interest in downtown Sonora. An old mercantile building is being remodeled to house shops, offices and boutiques. Travelers from elsewhere are apt to think this is far West Texas until they realize that Sonora is only the halfway point on the highway from Houston to El Paso. Sonora was late

1

1) An old stone store building at Main and Water streets in Sonora is being restored to its original appearance. The interior is being modernized to house shops, boutiques and offices. 2) The Caverns of Sonora offer guided tours every half hour, all day, every day. The Caverns are a few miles west of Sonora off I-10. There is a trailer park.

2

getting a railroad, but the town has always been on a main road. It was a stopping point on the early stage line. That line became U.S. Highway 290, and now it is Interstate 10. This is one of our busiest highways. There are estimates that one million travelers pass by or through Sonora every year.

The Caverns of Sonora are just off Interstate 10, about fifteen miles west of Sonora. There are guided tours every half hour, all day, every day. The guided tour takes about an hour and a half, and the limestone formations along the route are lighted with some imagination. Admission fees were three dollars for adults and two dollars for children when we were there last. There is a trailer park at the site.

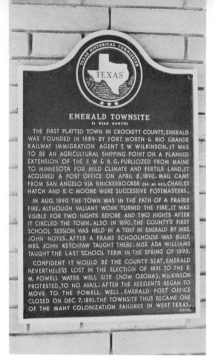

EMERALD TOWNSITE
(1 MILE NORTH)

THE FIRST PLATTED TOWN IN CROCKETT COUNTY, EMERALD WAS FOUNDED IN 1889· BY FORT WORTH & RIO GRANDE RAILWAY IMMIGRATION AGENT T. W. WILKINSON. IT WAS TO BE AN AGRICULTURAL SHIPPING POINT ON A PLANNED EXTENSION OF THE F. W. & R. G. PUBLICIZED FROM MAINE TO MINNESOTA FOR MILD CLIMATE AND FERTILE LAND, IT ACQUIRED A POST OFFICE ON APRIL 8, 1890. MAIL CAME FROM SAN ANGELO VIA KNICKERBOCKER (10 MI. N E). CHARLES HATCH AND E. C. MOORE WERE SUCCESSIVE POSTMASTERS.

IN AUG. 1890 THE TOWN WAS IN THE PATH OF A PRAIRIE FIRE. ALTHOUGH VALIANT WORK TURNED THE FIRE, IT WAS VISIBLE FOR TWO NIGHTS BEFORE AND TWO NIGHTS AFTER IT CIRCLED THE TOWN. ALSO IN 1890, THE COUNTY'S FIRST SCHOOL SESSION WAS HELD IN A TENT IN EMERALD BY MRS. JOHN NOYES. AFTER A FRAME SCHOOLHOUSE WAS BUILT, MRS. JOHN KETCHPAW TAUGHT THERE. MISS ADA WILLIAMS TAUGHT THE LAST SCHOOL TERM IN THE SPRING OF 1893.

CONFIDENT IT WOULD BE THE COUNTY SEAT, EMERALD NEVERTHELESS LOST IN THE ELECTION OF 1891 TO THE E. M. POWELL WATER WELL SITE (NOW OZONA). WILKINSON PROTESTED, TO NO AVAIL. AFTER THE RESIDENTS BEGAN TO MOVE TO THE POWELL WELL, EMERALD POST OFFICE CLOSED ON DEC. 7, 1891. THE TOWNSITE THUS BECAME ONE OF THE MANY COLONIZATION FAILURES IN WEST TEXAS.
(1978)

What was intended to be a town has become the world's fanciest truck stop. The first settlement in Crockett County was at this site. The town called Emerald was on its way to becoming the county seat. It was the only town in the county until another promoter established a town six and a half miles farther west. That town was Ozona and it became the county seat and everybody in Emerald moved to Ozona. Where Emerald was, the Circle Bar Truck Stop is now. The Emerald townsite marker is now attached to the comfortable motel millionaire Tom Mitchell has built at his huge truck stop on I-10. It is six and a half miles east of Ozona, and you do not have to be a trucker to stop here.

The freeways in some of our metropolitan areas have become nightmares, but I-10 in this part of the state is a joy to drive. It is also beautiful.

CROCKETT COUNTY

This county also is part of the Edwards plateau. It is a limestone table with a thin layer of soil on top. Most of Crockett County is ranches, but there is also substantial oil and gas production here.

The only town in the county is Ozona. The county was named for the Alamo hero David Crockett. The name of the county seat obviously was chosen by somebody enchanted by the climate. Ozona claims to have more millionaires per capita than any other city in the country.

There was no town at Ozona when the legislature created Crockett County in 1875. The only town in the county when it finally was organized in 1891 was Emerald. That town was about six and a half miles east of the present site of Ozona. Emerald was settled in 1888. The town had a school, a store and several homes. It was established at a time when land speculators were very active. Emerald had been laid out by a land speculator named T. A. Wilkinson, and he was out-promoted by a promoter named E. M. Powell. And Powell

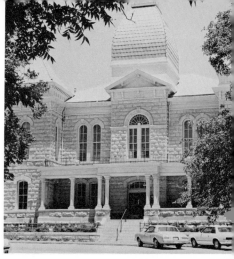

1) Ozona became the county seat of Crockett County in 1891. The present courthouse was built of native stone in 1902. It is the county's second courthouse. It cost only thirty thousand dollars and it is a recorded Texas and national landmark. 2) The Crockett County Museum in the courthouse annex on U.S. 290 in Ozona is open every afternoon except Monday. There are displays of Indian artifacts and relics of the frontier days.

had some help from the weather. He founded Ozona just in time to make it a contender in the election to establish the county seat. The election was held in 1891. There was a cloudburst in June of that year. The town of Emerald was flooded. The election was in July. Ozona was chosen to be the county seat.

The people of Emerald moved to Ozona. Some of them moved their houses. The school at Emerald closed in 1893. The building was moved to Ozona in 1897. It was used as a saloon, as a boarding house and as a garage at various times. Emerald lasted less than ten years.

Ozona has survived all these years without a railroad. The

1) The porch makes the old Crockett County Jail building in Ozona look almost homey. Quarters for the sheriff and his family were built in when the jail was built in 1892. The tower may have been designed to accommodate a scaffold for hangings, but no scaffold was ever installed. 2) The oldest house still standing in Ozona is one of those moved here from Emerald when Emerald folded up. It is a fairly typical early west Texas house, built in the 1890s. There are also many fine, big homes in Ozona because many of the prosperous owners of Crockett County ranches live in the city. It has been said that Ozona has more millionaires per capita than any other city, but this probably does not include Saudi Arabia.

2

railroad builders overlooked Crockett County almost entirely. The Santa Fe tracks pass through only the extreme western tip of the county. Ozona had to make do with stage lines connecting with the Southern Pacific at Comstock to the south, and with the Santa Fe at San Angelo to the north until about 1914. Buses and jitneys took over from the stage lines then.

There is a state marker at the stage stop where the coaches

1) The first bank in Ozona was the Ozona National. It was organized by a doctor and a group of ranchers and they built this building in 1905. It is a registered Texas landmark. 2) Its face has been lifted, probably more than once. But the Crockett Hotel was built in the 1890s. It was originally called the Ozona Hotel. Oil field workers and geologists lived here while they were developing the Crockett County oil fields in the early 1920s.

2

made their first change of horses on the road from Ozona to San Angelo. The marker is nine miles north of Ozona in a roadside park on State Highway 163. The stage stop here carried the poetically appropriate name of High Lonesome.

There is also a marker at the site of the town of Emerald. It is six and a half miles east of Ozona on U.S. 290.

The courthouse in Ozona was built in 1902. It is made of native stone, and it is listed in the *National Register of Historic Places*. This pretty well ensures that no future county commissioners will add aluminum windows or asphalt

1) The old original Ozona Hotel looks to be in better shape than this building, built to replace it, in 1926, and called the New Ozona Hotel. 2) The army's old Fort Lancaster is owned now by the State Department of Parks and Wildlife. The last soldier left here in 1871 and the fort has been in ruins for a long time. 3) The Parks Department has established a Visitors' Center at the site and there are displays here including some relics and artifacts found in the ruins.

shingles. The old jail building was built in 1892. The original Ozona Hotel on the square was built in 1893. The new Hotel Ozona was built in 1926. The Circle Bar Truck Stop on the highway outside Ozona is one of the fancier truckers' resorts in the country.

The oldest house in Ozona is the Deland home at Avenue F and Eleventh Street. It was moved here from Emerald in the 1890s and the Delands bought it in 1916. The old Ozona National Bank Building was built in 1905 at 910 Avenue E. The

From the top of the cliff east of Fort Lancaster you can see the scars made years ago by the locked wheels of coaches and wagons sliding down the trail toward the fort.

Crockett County Museum in the courthouse annex is open every afternoon except Monday. Exhibits trace the early history of the area. There is no admission charge, but donations are welcome.

Prehistoric Indians left some artifacts and rock paintings here. The Lipan Apaches occupied the area when the first Europeans came. They were displaced by the Comanches, and the Comanches were not subdued finally until the late 1870s. A marker at Howard's Well, thirty-six miles west of Ozona, recalls that a wagon train was wiped out here in April of 1872. Sixteen settlers were killed.

Howard's Well was a favorite watering hole of the Indians and it was also used by settlers and traders traveling the old Chihuahua trail between Chihuahua and the Texas coast.

The U.S. Army established Fort Lancaster on the Chihuahua trail in 1855. The site is on Live Oak Creek, one mile north of the point where the creek feeds into the Pecos River. Fort Lancaster also became a stopping point on the Southern Overland mail run from San Antonio to San Diego. Many of the immigrants heading for California came this way. Texas cattlemen were driving herds of longhorns to the California goldfields by this route as early as 1854. The U.S. Army's experimental camel caravan to California came through here in 1857.

The U.S. Army withdrew from Fort Lancaster when Texas

Millions of gallons of water gush from a cluster of springs north of the city of Del Rio every day. The springs supply the city's water and feed a system of irrigation canals built more than one hundred years ago. The irrigation system here may be the oldest one in the country still intact and still in use.

left the Union in 1861. There was a small U.S. garrison here again briefly in 1870 and 1871, but it never was fully manned again after 1861. The fort is in ruins. It probably will remain in ruins. Descendants of Howard and Alma Cox gave the property to the state in 1968. The State Department of Parks and Wildlife has established a visitors' center at the site. Artifacts found on the grounds are on display in the center. One or two of the other frontier forts have been restored. There are no present plans to restore this one.

The countryside around here has not changed much since the days of the stagecoaches and covered wagons, except that the road is vastly better. Some appreciation of what traveling conditions were like in those earlier days can be obtained by standing in the roadside park on the cliff east of Fort Lancaster. The scars made by the wheels of those coaches and wagons can still be seen on the rocky slope between here and the ruins of the fort. Drivers had to lock and tie their wheels, then hang on and hope as they descended to the valley floor. And imagine what the trip in the other direction, up this jumble of rocks, was like. Standing here on this ridge and looking down at the ruins of Fort Lancaster, you can appreciate the risks the early settlers accepted as a condition of life on the frontier.

VAL VERDE COUNTY

Val Verde County has some of the state's more spectacular scenery and some interesting history. Judge Roy Bean's old courthouse saloon is here. There is a state park. There is a major lake, and there are some ancient Indian rock paintings in Val Verde County.

This county was created and organized in 1885 from parts

The tourist shops in the Mexican city of Acuna across the river from Del Rio are clustered mostly along Hidalgo Street. Access to the international toll bridge is not as easy in Del Rio as it is in some border cities. The bridge is some distance from the main Del Rio business district by way of Garfield Avenue and Spur 239. There are parking lots at the Texas end of the bridge where you can leave your car and catch a bus or a taxi to the other side.

of Kinney, Pecos and Crockett counties. It was named for a Civil War battle.

The county seat from the beginning has been the city of Del Rio beside the Rio Grande. Del Rio grew from a settlement originally called San Felipe del Rio. The site was a natural choice because water was plentiful here long before the Amistad Dam was built in the 1960s. The San Felipe springs rise near the edge of the present city of Del Rio, and they feed San Felipe Creek and the creek feeds into the Rio Grande. The San Felipe springs produce prodigious quantities of water. The water gushes up out of the ground through openings as big as the wells the early settlers used to dig. But these holes were here long before the first settlers came. The flow is more than 90 million gallons a day. Some of the water is channeled into irrigation ditches. But there is more ranching than farming in the county as a whole, and Del Rio claims to be the wool and mohair capital of the world. (But San Angelo also claims to be.) There is also a little oil and gas production here, and catering to the tourists is a sizable industry.

There are two official crossing points on the border here, and no one knows how many unofficial crossing points. There is a toll bridge across the Rio Grande, below the dam, linking Del Rio directly with Ciudad Acuna on the Mexican side. There is also a free crossing on the dam itself. This road gives access directly to the park and recreation areas on the Texas and Mexican shores of Amistad Reservoir. It also connects on the Mexican side with a road that will take you south to Ciudad Acuna.

You can drive your car this far into Mexico without any kind of permit, but you should have Mexican insurance on

1) The Whitehead Memorial Museum is headquartered in an old building that was a trading post in the stagecoach days. There is a replica of Judge Roy Bean's old saloon and courthouse and the graves of Judge Bean and his son are both on the museum grounds. 2) The oldest bonded winery in Texas is still doing business on its original site in what is now a suburb of Del Rio. The Val Verde Vineyard and Winery was established in 1883, by the Qualia family and the same family still operates it.

the car. If you do not want to drive your own car into Mexico, there are parking places by the International Bridge at Del Rio where you can leave your car and take a taxi or bus or walk across to Ciudad Acuna. (See index for more information on crossing the border.)

The Whitehead Museum in Del Rio is in an old building at 1308 South Main that served as a trading post in earlier days. Exhibits in the museum recall the frontier days and the life and times of frontier Judge Roy Bean. The museum is open every day except Sunday. There is no admission fee.

The oldest winery in Texas is at 139 Hudson Drive here in Del Rio. It is the Val Verde Winery. It was established in 1883 and it is still operated by members of the founding family.

One of the more controversial figures of the twenties and

Dr. John Brinkley lived here in the 1930s when he was upsetting the U.S. medical profession by advertising his goat gland transplants on his very high powered radio station on the other side of the border. Brinkley's widow continued to live here until 1977. The Brinkley house is on Hudson Drive just a few blocks from the winery. It is not open to visitors.

thirties was Dr. John R. Brinkley. He set the medical world on its ear by implanting goat glands in human patients to make them friskier. Many of his patients sang his praises, but Brinkley was barred from practicing almost everywhere. For a time he lived in a fancy house on Hudson Drive in south Del Rio and broadcast his advice, philosophy and ads from a powerful radio station on the Mexican side of the river, beyond the reach of U.S. authorities. Brinkley's widow lived in the home here until 1977.

The courthouse in Del Rio was built in 1887. The old jail was built in 1885.

Several homes built around the turn of the century stand along Spring and Garfield streets here. The oldest home in Del Rio is at the corner of Pecan and Nicholson. This was originally a walled hacienda. It was built about 1863. The Sacred Heart Church at 310 Mill Street was built in 1892.

There are huge catfish in the Amistad Reservoir, and the Texas Department of Parks and Wildlife has been stocking the lake with game fish ever since the dam was completed in 1968. There are walleyes and striped bass, black bass and northern pike to be caught here. Two thirds of the lake is under Texas jurisdiction, and the other third is Mexican. Licenses for fishing on the Mexican side can be obtained in Ciudad Acuna, and at some of the sporting goods stores on the Texas side of the lake.

Amistad is one of the biggest artificial lakes in the state.

1

2

1) Val Verde County still has its original courthouse and jail building. There is a modern addition adjacent to the original courthouse built in 1887. 2) And there is a newer addition alongside the original jail built in 1885. 3) The Sacred Heart Catholic Church was built on Mill Street, facing the courthouse in 1892. It is a recorded Texas landmark. 4) The oldest house in Del Rio is the Donna Paula Losoya de Perez de Taylor de Rivers place at Nicholson and Pecan. It was built in 1863. The glass bricks around the entrance must have been added a good bit later. It is a private residence. Travelers in strange towns looking for something they want to see often stop and ask directions at service stations. It has been our experience that much better information can be obtained at fire stations.

3

4

1

2

1) The boundary markers on the Amistad Dam. Two thirds of the huge lake behind the Amistad Dam is in Texas, one third in Mexico. There is a highway across the top of the dam, and recreation areas at both ends. There is no toll. 2) Lake Amistad is clear, clean and the fishing is good. There is a marina at the Diablo East Recreation area off U.S. 90 and there are several campgrounds in the recreation areas maintained by the National Park Service.

The water is surprisingly clear. There are more than 850 miles of shoreline, and the lake backs up into some of the most beautiful canyons to be found anywhere. Limestone cliffs rise from the water's edge along the original course of the Rio Grande and the Devil's River.

Some of the earliest inhabitants of this area used the rock overhangs here for shelter thousands of years ago. Some of the rock walls here are still blackened by the smoke from their campfires. And there are pictures on the rock walls of these canyons painted by Indians hundreds and thousands of years ago. The state is developing a park in the Seminole Canyon, just below where the Pecos River runs into Lake Amistad.

1

3

1) Seminole Canyon is on the upper reaches of the big lake. The early inhabitants left some primitive and durable paintings on the walls of some of the rock shelters they used here. 2) Panther Cave takes its name from a large red painting of a panther still discernible on the wall here. Anybody with a boat can get to Panther Cave, so a fence has been put up to protect the Indian art. 3) Camping from boats is permitted around the shores of Lake Amistad. The water backs up into limestone canyons and the rock shelters used by ancient Indians.

2

NO CAMPING

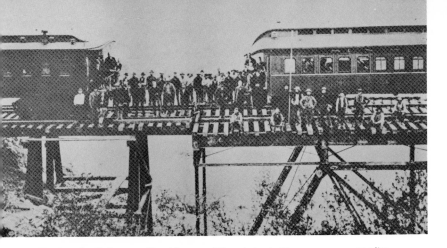

The line the Galveston, Harrisburg and San Antonio Company was extending westward from San Antonio met the line the Southern Pacific was extending eastward from California west of the Pecos River near Langtry in 1883. This is the driving of the last spike.

The Panther Cave at the mouth of this canyon has some outstanding examples of Indian rock paintings, including a very large red panther. The paintings in these canyons were relatively safe from vandals before the dam was built. Many of them are now easily accessible by boat, and some of the people able to reach them now, unfortunately, seem more interested in creating graffiti than they are in seeing the graffiti the early inhabitants left behind. Several of the canyons here are listed in the *National Register of Historic Places.*

The National Park Service has established six camping areas on the shores of Lake Amistad, and there are four public launching areas. You can get a brochure with more details from the Del Rio Chamber of Commerce at Box 1388, Del Rio, 78840.

The shoreline is open to unrestricted camping. But all the property above the 1,144 foot elevation is privately owned, so campers should not wander very far from their campsites.

Railroad history was made in Val Verde County when the railroad C. P. Huntington was building eastward from San Francisco met the road the Galveston, Harrisburg & San Antonio line was building westward from Houston. That happened here on the west bank of the Pecos River. One of the great construction feats of the railroad era was the building of the high bridge across the Pecos Canyon in 1892. Today's traveler can get a pretty good idea what kind of engineering triumph this was and what kind of hardships the earlier travelers endured from the lookout point at the east

The original railroad bridge across the Pecos was down close to the river. The railroad engineers realized they could shorten their line and eliminate the danger of flood damage by putting a bridge across the Pecos Canyon and in 1892 they finished work on what was then the highest bridge in the world. This original high bridge was dismantled in 1947 and moved to Guatemala after its replacement was built. Jimmy Doolittle reportedly flew a small airplane under the old high bridge in the 1920s.

end of the bridge that now carries U.S. Highway 90 over the Pecos River. And the traveler should remember that the canyon was substantially deeper then than it appears today, because the Amistad Dam has backed water up in this part of the Pecos to a depth of about one hundred feet.

The most famous resident this part of the state ever had was a man named Roy Bean. He was born in Kentucky, and he settled in San Antonio about the time the Civil War ended. Bean started operating a kind of portable saloon as the railroad builders pushed westward. He was running his saloon in a tent in a camp called Vinegarroon in the Pecos country in 1882 when the rangers and the railroad people decided there was a need for some kind of justice to discourage lawlessness. Roy Bean was chosen justice of the peace. The kind of justice he dealt out made him a legend. Bean began his judicial career in Vinegarroon, but he made most of his reputation in a town he always claimed was named for an English music hall queen. That town was Langtry. Bean moved his saloon and court to a frame building here when the east and west sections of the railroad finally were joined nearby. Bean was a fan of the English entertainer Lillie Langtry. She was also known as the Jersey Lily. He named his saloon the Jersey Lilly, and he said he

1) *Judge Roy Bean held court and sold beer and whiskey in this little frame building directly across from the depot in Langtry. The Texas Department of Highways and Public Transportation has built a Visitors' Center around the old Bean courthouse. 2) Bean's colorful and original interpretations of the law made him a legend on the frontier.*

2

named the town for Miss Langtry, but the rest of the evidence suggests the town was actually named for one of the foremen on the Southern Pacific project. The name of the saloon has always been spelled Jersey Lilly, although Miss Langtry spelled her stage name with only one *l*.

Roy Bean was the Law West of the Pecos until he died in 1904. The State Highway Department has developed a visitors' center around Bean's old saloon. It is on Loop 25 off U.S. 90 at Langtry. It is open every day, except for three days at Christmastime. There is no admission charge, and the features include an extensive cactus garden.

Bean's notoriety hit its peak in 1896 when he staged a world championship heavyweight fight. Authorities in Texas and Mexico had prohibited the fight, but Bean outsmarted them by staging it on a sandbar on the Mexican side of the Rio Grande. There were no Mexican authorities on hand to prevent the fight and the Texas Rangers had no authority in the area where it was held. Bob Fitzsimmons knocked out Peter Maher in less than three minutes and Fitzsimmons claimed the world championship that Jim Corbett had abdicated in favor of Maher.

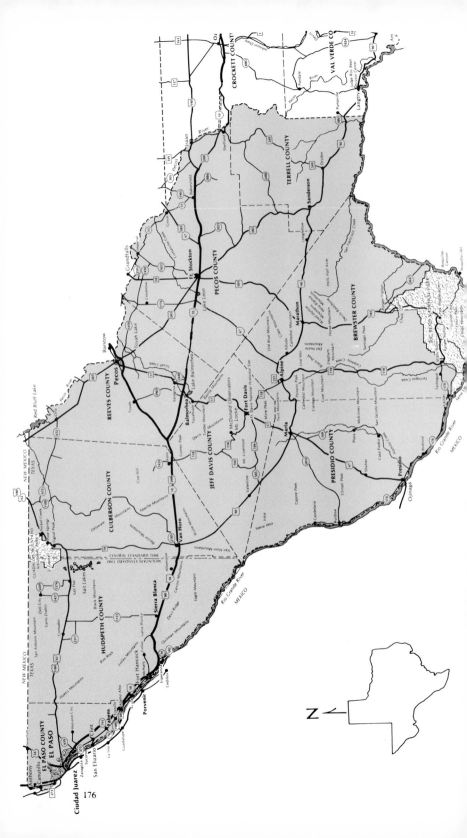

West of the Pecos

*Terrell, Pecos, Brewster, Presidio, Jeff
Davis, Reeves, Culberson, Hudspeth, El
Paso counties*

One of the legendary stage lines of the frontier days ran
through this picturesque country. Some of the most famous
military men in the history of our nation served here. The
final link in one of the earliest transcontinental rail lines was
forged here. The Comanche War Trail passed this way. This
is a land of mirages and mountains, a land of deserts and
oases. This is the land most people elsewhere see in their
minds' eye when they think of Texas. This is the Texas of the
western novels and the western movies.

The Butterfield Overland mail line started carrying
passengers and mail from St. Louis to San Francisco in
September of 1858. The route through Texas was between
Colbert's Ferry on the Oklahoma border and El Paso, then
called Franklin, on the New Mexico border.

The Butterfield line's Concord coaches reached the Pecos
River at Horsehead Crossing about twenty miles northwest of
the present town of Girvin in Pecos County. The drivers
originally went up the east or the west bank of the Pecos from
here, depending upon their preferences and road conditions,
to the Emigrant Crossing near the present city of Pecos, in
Reeves County. The road followed the river northward then
to Pope's Camp, six miles northwest of the present town of
Orla in Reeves County, and then it traveled due west to the
Hueco tanks and on into El Paso. The Butterfield trail joined

1

1) Most of Terrell County still has the appearance of the frontier. It is a large area with a small population. Most of the county is in ranches, raising cattle, sheep and goats. The only major highway in the county is U.S. 90, paralleling the Southern Pacific tracks. 2) A. W. Terrell was a lawyer and a district judge in Austin before the Civil War. He rose to the rank of brigadier general in the Confederate army. He later served in the legislature. This county is named for him.

with the California emigrant trail at Emigrant Crossing, and these two trails followed the same route from Emigrant Crossing on west. The route was changed in late 1858 to a more direct line from Horsehead Crossing through Fort Stockton to El Paso. This was the same route the stage line between San Antonio and El Paso was using.

The Goodnight-Loving cattle trail followed part of the route of the Butterfield stage. Cattlemen Charles Goodnight and Oliver Loving blazed this trail in 1866 driving their cattle to market in New Mexico.

The Comanche War Trail was the route the Comanche Indians used in moving between their camps in Mexico and their hideouts in the high plains and panhandle sections of Texas. The trail passed through Comanche Springs, where Fort Stockton is today. It branched south of Comanche Springs with one leg crossing the Rio Grande at Boquillas in the present Big Bend National Park, and the other leg crossing the border farther upstream. The trail ran northeastward from Comanche Springs through Big Spring.

TERRELL COUNTY
Terrell County was part of the original Presidio County. It

Terrell County was not created until 1905. The Southern Pacific railroad line had been completed by that time and there were two settlements on the rail line in this county, both established because of the railroad while the area was still part of Pecos County. Sanderson became the county seat when the county was formed in 1905. The courthouse was built in 1908.

was formed in 1905 from part of Pecos County, after Pecos County had been split off from Presidio County. Terrell County is named for General A. W. Terrell. He was a fellow with a really varied background. If people had been writing resumés in his day, his resumé would have been a corker. Terrell came to Texas in 1852 with a law degree. He practiced law in Austin until the Civil War got started. He got a commission as a second lieutenant in the Confederate army and won a series of promotions. He was a brigadier general when the war ended. Terrell went to Mexico after Lee surrendered the Confederate forces, and for a while, he served as an officer in the army trying to keep the foreign emperor Maximilian in power. He served in the legislature after he returned to Texas and then Grover Cleveland named him minister to Turkey in 1893. Terrell was the first to propose that jurors in Texas ought to be able to read and write. He got that idea approved by the legislature while he was a member. Terrell lived to be eighty-five. He died in Mineral Wells in 1912.

The county seat of Terrell County is the town of Sanderson, on Sanderson Creek in the western end of the county. The present courthouse was built in 1908. The town grew out of a settlement originally called Strawbridge and the reason it is here, is that the first settlers knew this spot was going to be

The other landmark on the square in Sanderson is St. James Catholic Church. This part of west Texas is subject to sudden floods. Cloudbursts upstream can fill up a normally dry creek and send a wall of water roaring down on towns and ranches and highway travelers with very little warning. But Sanderson has survived. The town also survived a lot of rustlers, gunmen and adventurers who congregated here in the 1880s, partly because of rumors of a lost gold mine. If there is such a mine, it is still lost.

on the first rail line to be built in this part of the world. Roy Bean operated his traveling saloon here for a time during the building of the railroad. Sanderson has survived several devastating floods.

The only other town on the map of Terrell County is Dryden. It is on U.S. Highway 90 and on the Texas and New Orleans rail line, as Sanderson is. Dryden was another settlement that developed mostly because the site was on the route chosen by the first railroad builders.

Myers Spring, in southern Terrell County, was a popular Indian watering hole. The spring is about fifteen miles northeast of Dryden. There are rock shelters with primitive paintings done by the Comanches and Apaches. They used to camp around here before and during the early days of white settlement. Myers Spring was also a base from 1880 until 1882 for the U.S. Army's Seminole Indian Scouts and their leader, John Bullis. Bullis' scouts played a major role in Ranald Mackenzie's final successful campaigns against the west Texas Indian tribes. The Texas legislature commended Bullis in 1882 for "his efforts in repelling the depredations of the In-

Dryden is the other town on the railroad line in Terrell County. It was named for railroad man Gene Dryden, when the route for the tracks was laid out in 1880. It probably seemed like a good idea at the time to have a town here. But Dryden is not flourishing. This oil well apparently never amounted to much, either, but there is substantial oil production elsewhere in Terrell County.

dians.'' Myers Spring is listed in the *National Register of Historic Places* because of the pictographs in the rock shelters, but it is on private property. Bullis went on from his frontier experiences to serve with Teddy Roosevelt in Cuba during the Spanish-American War. He retired from the army as a brigadier general and he died in San Antonio in 1911. A World War I training base in San Antonio, later incorporated into Fort Sam Houston, was named for John Bullis. General Bullis' collection of Indian relics and artifacts is in the Witte Museum in San Antonio.

There is some oil and gas production in Terrell County, but the economy still is based mostly upon ranching.

Your great-grandmother's old kerosene range probably had little peep holes in the door, covered with a transparent material she probably called isinglass. It was actually mica, shaved into thin sheets, and it may have come from here. There were mica mines in this area, and one of the canyons U.S. Highway 90 crosses, west of Sanderson, is still called Isinglass Canyon.

The Rio Grande forms the southern boundary of Terrell County, but there are no official border crossing points listed on the map.

1) Fort Stockton was a fort before it was a town. The army established the fort here in 1859 as part of the chain of forts to protect settlers and travelers and discourage the Comanches from raiding into Mexico. The army abandoned the fort in 1886 but some of the buldings are still standing. The old stone guardhouse still has the leg irons in the prisoners' cell. 2) The old officers' quarters at the fort have been turned into private residences.

PECOS COUNTY

This is the second biggest county in Texas. It is almost as large as the state of Connecticut. Only Brewster County is bigger. Pecos and Brewster counties both were split off from Presidio County in the 1870s after the original Presidio County was split off from the Bexar District in 1850. Pecos County was organized in 1872, with Fort Stockton as the county seat. The first courthouse was built in 1881 on the same site where the present courthouse stands. The present courthouse was built in 1912.

Also on the courthouse square or plaza are the Catholic church, built in 1871, and an old school house built in 1883. One of the earliest Anglo settlers here was Peter Gallagher. He was an Irishman, and the settlement he founded outside of

1) There was a big spring here in the early days. It was a regular stopping point on the Comanche War Trail before the first Europeans came, so it was called Comanche Springs. The spring has stopped flowing, now, but there is a large swimming pool where it was. 2) This town started out as a trading post outside the fort. It was originally called St. Gall. The name was changed to Fort Stockton when the town became the county seat. The courthouse was built in 1912.

2

the U.S. Army's Fort Stockton was originally called St. Gall. The settlement took the name of the fort after the county was organized, and the settlement was designated the county seat.

The army established Fort Stockton in 1859, well before Pecos County was organized. The fort was built beside a major watering hole that had been called Comanche Springs. The old Comanche War Trail running north and south from the border to the panhandle passed by the springs and the stagecoach route between San Antonio and San Diego was laid out in 1857 to take advantage of this water hole.

The fort was established to protect the stage line. The U.S. Army withdrew the garrison at the beginning of the Civil War, but troops returned here in 1867, and the fort remained active until it was finally abandoned in 1886. Some of the buildings are still here, on Williams Street between Fourth and Fifth streets. The surviving guardhouse and three officers' quarters are listed in the *National Register of Historic Places*.

Some of the earliest Spanish explorers, probably including

1) St. Joseph's Catholic Church was completed in 1875 on land dedicated for the purpose in the original plat of St. Gall townsite. The name St. Gall was invented by the original civilian settler, Peter Gallagher, apparently in honor of himself. Fort Stockton was named for Commodore Robert Stockton, a hero of the war with Mexico. 2) The original Fort Stockton school building was built in 1883. It is now a day care center.

Cabeza de Vaca, camped at Comanche Springs. The early Indians knew they could always find water here. The springs were flowing freely in the pioneer days, and some of the early settlers tapped the springs for irrigation water.

Early traveler N. A. Taylor wrote in his journal *Two Thousand Miles in Texas on Horseback* that Fort Stockton looked like another Eden when he visited here in 1877. He said he found rich gardens, irrigated farms and a garrison of six companies of Negro soldiers with white officers at the fort. The springs here were flowing 60 million gallons of water a day then. The water supply seemed inexhaustible. But it was not. The Comanche Springs are no longer flowing. The city of Fort Stockton has built a park at the site, though, with a large swimming pool. A water festival is staged here in the James Rooney Park on the third weekend in July. There is substantial farming and ranching here, but the oil and gas wells earn most of the county's income.

Pecos County was one of those places where the sheepmen and the cowmen got substantially in each other's way. The cowmen wanted to run their stock on the open ranges and the sheepmen wanted to fence the cows out of their pastures.

1) Old Fort Stockton had its share of badmen and gamblers and one of the places they and other thirsty people congregated in the frontier days was the Grey Mule Saloon. The old watering hole is now a private residence. 2) The oldest house in Fort Stockton is growing older and not very gracefully. It was built sometime before 1859.

2

There was a time in Fort Stockton when saloons, stores and gambling houses catered either to cowmen or to sheepmen, and the proprietors hoped they would never have people from the two factions in their establishments at the same time. But there were no really violent clashes between cowmen and sheepmen here as there were in Tom Green, San Saba and Kimball counties.

One of those early saloons is still standing in Fort Stockton. The old Grey Mule Saloon at Callaghan and Main has been restored to something probably better than the condition it was in, in the late 1800s.

The oldest house in town is an adobe place at 201 W. Sherrer Street.

The old Annie Riggs Hotel at 301 South Main Street has been turned into a museum.

This is another adobe building. Mrs. Annie Riggs operated a hotel here in the early 1900s, catering to cowboys and politicians. The museum in the old building has displays depicting

1

1) Mrs. Annie Riggs operated a hotel in this big adobe building in the early 1900s. Her customers were ranchers, cowboys, politicians and assorted travelers and some of them were a bit rowdy. But Mrs. Riggs was described as a quiet and cultured lady. This is now a museum. 2) Some of the leading citizens of Fort Stockton decided in 1894 that the county sheriff had to go. He turned up dead very shortly thereafter. The killer never was identified. The grave marker says only that he was assassinated. 3) The Butterfield Overland Stage Line originally followed the Pecos River but was soon changed to follow the line of fortifications on the way to California. There was a stage stop 20 miles east of Fort Stockton where the coaches changed horses. The Highway Department rebuilt the stage stop at a rest stop on I-10.

2

3

1

1) Prehistoric beasts walked here. These dinosaur tracks are in a county park 22 miles northeast of Fort Stockton on U.S. 67. They call it Dinosaur Park. 2) The presence of dinosaur tracks in the neighborhood probably inspired cartoonist V. T. Hamlin to invent his stone-age comic strip hero Alley Oop. Hamlin was living in Iraan when he started doing that strip. There is a Fantasyland Park in honor of Hamlin and Oop here. Iraan is at the eastern edge of Pecos County.

2

frontier life and some of the history of the county and the cattle business. The museum is open every day except Wednesday. There is no fixed admission fee, but donations are solicited.

There is an old army cemetery in Fort Stockton, but the bodies of the dead soldiers originally buried here were all moved to Fort Sam Houston in San Antonio when Fort Stockton was abandoned. A number of other graves remain in the old fort cemetery, though. One tombstone here marks the grave of former Sheriff A. J. Royal. Apparently he was too high handed for the community. They say that six of the town's leading citizens met in 1894 and decided Sheriff Royal

1) The Iraan Museum in the Alley Oop Park has some historical displays dealing with the town and the prolific Yates Oil Field discovered in 1926. 2) The Yates Field here was producing so much oil by 1928 that a system of voluntary proration was adopted to protect the price of Texas crude. Pecos County claims the world's largest gas well and the world's largest oil well. And the seismologists and geologists are still exploring here.

had to go. The six citizens drew beans from a hat that contained five white beans and one black bean. The citizen drawing the black bean was to do away with the sheriff. Royal was shot to death a short time later and his killer never was identified. The inscription on the tombstone records that Royal was assassinated in 1894. He was thirty-nine when he died. The climate here is regarded as a healthful one, but all of the people buried here in the old fort cemetery died or were killed before they were forty.

The old Butterfield Overland stagecoaches used to stop at Tunis Springs to change horses and drivers and to let the passengers refresh themselves. Tunis Springs was east of the present site of Fort Stockton. The stagecoach station was a couple of miles south of the present route of U.S. 290/I-10. But the old Tunis Springs station has been dismantled, moved and reassembled at a rest stop on U.S. 290, twenty miles east of Fort Stockton.

Pecos County has established a park outside of Fort Stockton to preserve and protect some prehistoric animal tracks. It is called Dinosaur Park, and it is twenty-two miles northeast of Fort Stockton on U.S. Highway 67.

The presence of these prehistoric animal tracks here may have helped inspire cartoonist V. T. Hamlin to invent the comic strip character Alley Oop. Hamlin was living in Iraan when he created Alley, his girlfriend Oola and his pet

The Horsehead Crossing on the Pecos River as it appears today. The Red Bluff Dam on the upper Pecos changed the character of the river considerably. It is usually shallow, now, but in the stagecoach days, the river along here was often one hundred feet wide and ten or twelve feet deep. Travelers had to be very careful where they crossed. It sometimes took days for a large wagon train to get across the Pecos.

dinosaur, Dinny.

All of this is commemorated in a fantasyland display adjacent to the city park in Iraan. There is also a museum in Iraan recalling some of the history of the area and the great oil strike of 1928. The museum is open every day except Monday and Tuesday during the summer months. It is open on weekends during the spring and fall, and it is closed during the winter. There is no admission charge, but donations are welcome. The park and museum are on State Highway 29 in Iraan, and there is a state marker at the site of the Yates Oil Field Discovery Well, at the Marathon Oil Company office on Highway 29. This town has nothing whatever in common with Persia except oil. The name is not Iran, but Iraan, and it is pronounced *ira-ann* for the very good reason that the town was founded by Ira and Ann Yates. The city park here has provisions for camping, picnicking and swimming.

Another historic spot in Pecos County is the Horsehead Crossing on the Pecos River, used by the stagecoaches and the immigrants' wagon trains a hundred years ago. There is a marker on Farm Road 11, ten miles north of Girvin in eastern Pecos County.

BREWSTER COUNTY

Brewster County is the biggest county in Texas. It has some of the most spectacular scenery. It includes the splendid Big

1) *There is a quiet county park and swimming pool today where the army had the fort it called Pena Colorado in the 1880s. The site would have been a logical location for the town of Marathon. But the Southern Pacific railroad laid its tracks a little farther north. Marathon was established beside the tracks in 1882. Fort Pena Colorado was abandoned in 1883.*
2) *The Chambers Hotel was one of the early buildings in Marathon. Ranchers stopped here when they brought their cattle to the railroad. It is faced with siding, now, but the basic building is adobe. The Chambers Hotel is now a private residence.*

2

Bend National Park.

Brewster County was created in 1887 from part of Presidio County. The state legislature actually meant to establish three counties in the area that Brewster County occupies, but the other two counties never materialized, and the entire area became Brewster County. It is larger than the entire state of Connecticut. Gold, silver and quicksilver were mined here in earlier days.

The county is named for Henry P. Brewster. He came to Texas from South Carolina in 1836, in time to fight for Texas at San Jacinto. Brewster later became private secretary to Sam Houston. He served as secretary of war for the Republic of Texas during the term of President David Burnet. He later was attorney general of the state of Texas, and he was a

1) *The guayule is a gray-colored shrub with tiny flowers. Rubber can be produced from its bark, and for a time it was, here in Marathon.* 2) *A factory was built beside the railroad tracks in Marathon in 1909 to produce rubber from the guayule. It operated off and on until it closed down in 1926 after changing hands several times. The government experimented with guayule again briefly during World War II before the formula for synthetic rubber was developed. The main trouble was that the bushes did not produce very much rubber and did not grow back after they were cut.* 3) *Part of the guayule rubber factory was dismantled after 1926 and part of it fell down and this is all that is left today.*

colonel in the Confederate army during the Civil War. Brewster died in 1884, before Brewster County was created.

Indian artifacts are still being found around the town of Marathon in north central Brewster County. The army established a fort here in 1880 as part of the defense against the Indians. It was called Fort Pena Colorado. The town of Marathon was established when the railroad came through in 1882. The fort was abandoned in 1893, but the town of Marathon endured. It is a trading center and shipping point for ranchers in this part of Brewster County. Marathon also gets a lot of tourist business. It is one of the gateways to the Big Bend National Park. The park is about eighty miles south of here by way of U.S. 385. Rockhounds come here to explore the Great Marathon Basin.

The Black Gap Wildlife Management Area between Marathon and the Big Bend National Park is a game preserve covering around 100,000 acres. Hunting is sometimes allowed in the management area, and fishing is permitted in the waters of the Rio Grande, and is said to be very good. The Black

1) The old Marathon railroad depot has been moved away from the tracks to a new location and it will be restored as a museum. The town was named by early settler A. E. Shepard. He had done some traveling and he thought the terrain here resembled the plains of Marathon in Greece. 2) Mule deer live a sheltered life in the Black Gap Wildlife Management Area but some hunting is permitted here. Sportsmen may hunt doves and quail here during specified periods by just paying a small fee at the management area office.

Gap Wildlife Area is on Ranch Road 2627, off U.S. 385, about fifty-five miles south of Marathon.

The county seat of Brewster County is the city of Alpine. This is the home of Sul Ross State University and another gateway to the Big Bend National Park. Alpine has had several other names. The site was one familiar to the earliest Indian inhabitants of this area. There is a natural spring here. The early Spanish explorers knew it as Alsate's Waterhole. The name was changed to Kokernot Spring when the Kokernot family acquired the land. The spring itself is part of the Kokernot Spring Park, now administered by Sul Ross State University. The settlement that grew up around the spring was being called Osborne when the Southern Pacific Railroad reached here in 1882. The railroad made the settlement a train

1) Sul Ross State University, founded in Alpine in 1920, was named for Lawrence Sullivan Ross. He was governor of Texas from 1887 to 1891 and president of A & M after that. Ross was in command of the Texas Ranger Company that recaptured Cynthia Ann Parker in 1860. 2) There is an excellent museum on the grounds of Sul Ross University. It looks like a very modest place from the outside, but there are several rooms full of exhibits and photographs on the lower level.

1

2

stop, and the name was changed to Murphyville in honor of Dan Murphy. He was the owner of the spring at the time. The name was changed to Alpine in 1888, and it has been Alpine ever since. The mountains apparently inspired the name.

The county courthouse at 200 6th Street was built in 1887. Some of the other buildings in Alpine with state historical markers are:

- The Carr-Bob Slight house at 406 North Fifth Street.
- The Gage-Van Sickle house at 109 North Third Street.
- The Ritchey Hotel at 102 E. Murphy Street.

The Museum of the Big Bend at the Sul Ross State University in Alpine features a stagecoach, assorted Indian artifacts and replicas of a general store and blacksmith shop. The museum is open every afternoon except Mondays. There is a

Sul Ross University now administers the small park surrounding the spring that attracted the first settlers to Alpine. Kokernot Spring was originally called Alsate's Waterhole. The earliest Spanish explorers were familiar with it and so were the Indians. The spring is on State Highway 223, north of the city.

small admission charge. The Apache Trading Post on U.S. 90 west of Alpine can furnish information on backpacking and raft trips. The mailing address is Box 997, Alpine, 79830. The Chihuahuan Desert Research Institute, Box 1334, Alpine, 78930, conducts occasional field seminars and camping trips in this area.

Texas Highway 118 runs southward out of Alpine to the Big Bend National Park on the border. About fifteen miles south of Alpine on Highway 118 is the Woodward Agate Ranch. Several varieties of agate are found here, and it is a rockhound resort. The ranch has campsites and trailer connections, and rock collectors are encouraged to stop and wander over the 4,000 acres of the ranch. There is a fee for the campsites, and they charge you by the pound for any rocks you carry away with you.

The Big Bend National Park is about a hundred miles south of Alpine. The park covers more than 700,000 acres, and it includes mountains, deserts and part of the Rio Grande valley. There are more than 100 miles of paved roads here, 150 miles of dirt roads, and hundreds of miles of hiking trails. The park has four campgrounds and two trailer parks and a lodge. Information and maps are available at the park headquarters. The park is open the year around. Anyone planning to stay overnight or for an extended period at the lodge should make reservations in advance with the National Park Concession, Inc., Big Bend National Park, Texas 79834.

Six sites in the Big Bend National Park are listed in the

1) *The courthouse at Alpine is one of the old ones. It was built in 1887. It is the original. This town originally was called Osborne. The name was changed to Murphyville in 1882 when the railroad came through. The name was changed to Alpine shortly after Brewster County was organized and this community was designated the county seat in 1887. 2) One of the older buildings in Alpine is the Gage-Van Sickle house at 109 North Third Street. The place has been modernized, but this is an adobe building. It was the home of some prominent early citizens and it is still a private residence.*

2

National Register of Historic Places. These include the site of the old Castolon army compound from the days of the Mexican revolution, the hot springs where J. O. Langford developed a health resort in the early 1900s, the Mariscal Mine where mercury once was dug out of the ground, and the sites of the old James Sublett and Homer Wilson ranches. Grass was much more plentiful here once. The ranges were overgrazed during World War I, and the area has never fully recovered.

Geologists say the Big Bend area was under water 100 million years ago. Dinosaurs lived here about the same time.

1) One of Alpine's recorded land-marks is about to fall down. This was the Ritchey Hotel in the frontier days. Subsequent owners put on the frame and shingle additions, but you still can see the original adobe walls on the ground floor. The location is 102 East Murphy Street. 2) The Apache Trading Post on U.S. 90 on the western edge of Alpine is not old and it is unlikely you will see any Apaches here. But this is one of the places you can get information about guides and equipment for raft and float trips through the canyons of the Rio Grande.

The pterodactyl was the biggest flying creature that ever lived anywhere, as far as we know. It had a wingspan of fifty-one feet. You won't see any pterodactyls here today, but there are 350 kinds of birds in the Big Bend park, and more than a thousand different kinds of plants. Mountain lions, deer, javelinas, coyotes and raccoons abound here, too. This is the west the way it was before airplanes and freeways.

One of the storied ghost towns of Texas is right outside the Big Bend National Park here in Brewster County. It is Ter-lingua on Farm Road 170, just west of the park. Cinnabar was discovered here in the late 1800s. Mercury comes from cinnabar. Mercury is also known as quicksilver. This was

1

1) The Woodward Agate Ranch is a resort for rockhounds. Frank Woodward charges them 35 cents a pound for the rocks. 2) The Big Bend National Park covers seven hundred thousand acres. 3) Its development started when the state of Texas designated part of this area a state park in 1933. The park was enlarged and taken over by the National Park Service in 1944.

2

3

1

1) *The lodge adjacent to the Big Bend Park headquarters in the Chisos Basin is built like a motel. There were some individual cabins here, too, but they are being torn down. So you need to make reservations well in advance unless you are bringing your own tent, trailer or RV. The phone number is 915-477-2291. 2) If you want to see Big Bend from horseback, you can arrange it with the Chisos Remuda, near the lodge in the Chisos Basin. What concessionaire Lynn Carter offers is guided tours. You cannot rent a horse and ride off by yourself. You can get information and make reservations by calling 915-477-2374.*

2

known as the Terlingua Quicksilver District in the early 1900s when there were several operators working mines here.

A Yankee financier named Howard E. Perry acquired some land here in 1887. It is not entirely clear whether Perry took the land in payment of a debt or bought it at a tax sale. And it is not clear whether he was aware of the quicksilver deposits when he acquired the land. But it is clear that he exploited them shrewdly after he became aware of them. Perry formed the Chisos Mining Company. He put an experienced mining engineer named W. B. Phillips in charge of the company, and the quicksilver they produced helped Perry maintain a fancy home on the coast of Maine and a couple of yachts. Perry did not spend much time at the mines, but he built a Moorish mansion on a ridge overlooking Terlingua. It is a picturesque ruin today, the most photogenic relic of the quicksilver days.

1

2

3

1) This is what Santa Elena Canyon looked like after a flood in the spring of 1979 deposited several feet of silt on the hiking trail. 2) The road to Santa Elena is the road to Castolon, past Castolon Peak. 3) There were mercury mines in the hills west of Big Bend in the late 1800s and early 1900s. A Yankee businessman named Howard Perry bought up some of the mines and established the Chisos Mining Company at Terlingua. The mines have been closed for nearly forty years and Perry's mansion is one of the ruins in the ghost town.

The cost of recovering and processing the cinnabar ore and getting it to market increased over the years, and the amount of ore recovered decreased until the operation became unprofitable. Perry went bankrupt during World War II. Another company tried operating the mines briefly, but that company went under, too, and the mines and the town were

1) The railroads never laid any tracks to Terlingua. It took some very sturdy wagons and a lot of sturdy mules to get Perry's mercury to the railroad at Alpine. Getting supplies and heavy equipment the 78 miles from Alpine to the mine was sometimes more difficult. 2) One of the old mines outside Terlingua has been turned into a motel. Some of the buildings here are new. Some of them were built originally by the mining company. 3) This is an authentic old border trading post. The trading post was about all that was here for a long time. But Lajitas has been discovered by a developer from Houston now.

3

abandoned about 1945.

Once a year there is a chili cook-off here. Between times, a company called Far Flung Adventures operates raft expeditions from Terlingua. A geologist named Glenn Pepper has

If it happens there is a heavy rain falling, you may not want to take State Highway 170 from Lajitas to Presidio. Runoff from the canyons along this road can get deep and swift anytime there is much rain and the road can become impassable. Any other time, this is the way to go.

developed a rustic motel and resort around one of the abandoned mine sites on Farm Road 170 between Terlingua and Lajitas. Bob Burleson of the Texas Explorers' Club publishes a booklet: *Suggested River Trips.* It is a canoeists' guide to this part of the state. Burleson will send you a copy if you send $4.25 to him at Box 844, Temple, 76501.

The tiny village of Lajitas has been discovered by a Houston promoter. There is a new motel and condominiums are springing up around the ancient trading post and cantina. Farm Road 170 is one of the most scenic drives in the United States. It parallels the Rio Grande northwestward from here to Presidio and beyond. If you are going to Presidio, take this route.

PRESIDIO COUNTY

Presidio County was created in 1870 and then reduced to the present size when Reeves, Pecos, Jeff Davis and Brewster counties were formed from parts of the original Presidio County. Presidio still is one of the biggest counties in the state in area.

If you are entering Presidio County from the Big Bend Park, you will travel up Farm Road 170 to Presidio. This picturesque route is called the Camino Del Rio. It takes you by Fort Leaton State Park. This is one of the state's Class V

1) Highway 170 passes some of the best mountain scenery in the state as it follows the canyon of the Rio Grande. 2) But it is not rock canyon all the way. There are fertile valleys along this section of the Rio Grande, too, where commercial farms grow big crops of onions, among other crops.

parks. There is no entrance fee. The main feature is the old building called Fort Leaton. It never was an actual military fort. It was a fortified trading post, acquired about 1848 and enlarged by a settler named Ben Leaton. It may have been built originally by the Spanish, as a mission, in the 1600s. Some accounts say this is the largest adobe building ever built. This may not be true, but it is one of the larger such buildings still standing. The fort is listed in the *National Register of Historic Places.* The Texas Department of Parks and Wildlife acquired the old building in 1968 and rebuilt it with adobe bricks made the same way the early settlers made them. There are several exhibits here recalling the way people lived in the west in earlier times. The park is about three miles east of the town of Presidio.

1) Round holes like this in the limestone formations along the Rio Grande apparently were used by the very early Indians for grinding the grain or seeds they used for food. 2) This is the Fort Leaton Park, now. It may have been a mission before a settler named Ben Leaton acquired it in 1848. It never was actually a fort, but it was a kind of fortified trading post and people got into the habit of calling it Fort Leaton. There are some exhibits inside, and there is no fee.

2   1

Presidio County takes its name from the town of Presidio, and the town takes its name from an old settlement on the Mexican side of the river. The Mexican settlement was La Junta, and it was also known as Presidio del Norte, or Fort of the North. There has been some form of farming going on in the valley of the Rio Grande here for more than three hundred years. The round holes the early Indians hollowed out in the rocks to grind their grain in are still to be found in many areas here.

The town across the Rio Grande from Presidio today is Ojinaga. There is the usual toll bridge linking the two cities and the usual rules on border crossings apply. The Chihuahua

1) Crumbling stone walls are scattered all over the hilly area beside Cibolo Creek where a big silver discovery was made in 1882. A prospector told General William Shafter about the discovery and the general borrowed some money and started a mining company. Shafter is a ghost town, now, but geologists and mining engineers are looking at the area again. 2) The mesquite has a very large root system and the pioneers sometimes would have been without firewood except for the mesquite roots. The beans of the mesquite are edible, too, and they were eaten by the early Indians before they knew anything about grain. Cows and horses eat them, too.

al Pacifico Railroad used to run passenger trains from Ojinaga to Los Mochis on the Pacific coast. The trains no longer run to Ojinaga, but you can drive or take the bus from Ojinaga to Chihuahua and catch the Chihuahua al Pacifico there. The train trip takes a little over twelve hours. The tracks pass over twenty-seven bridges and through seventy-three tunnels on the way through Copper Canyon and the Sierra Madre. The scenery is great and a first class ticket, one way, will cost you less than six dollars. You can get the train schedule and more information by writing to Chihuahua al Pacifico, P.O. Box 46, Chihuahua, Chihuahua, Mexico, or check with the travel agencies in Presidio.

If the name Presidio sounds familiar, it is because you have heard it mentioned so often in the TV weather reports as the hottest spot in Texas. The highest waterfall in the state is here on Capote Creek in Presidio County. Capote Falls are off Farm Road 170 near Candelaria. But they are on private property and not open to the public.

U.S. Highway 67 runs northward from Presidio to the county seat at Marfa. About twenty miles north of Presidio, Highway 67 passes by Old Shafter. It is a ghost town today, but Shafter once was ranked as one of the most productive

Fort D. A. Russell on the southern edge of Marfa was a cavalry post in the early 1900s. It was a training base during both world wars and it was a camp for German prisoners of war during the last two years of World War II. Some of the old buildings have been turned into comfortable homes and apartments, but many of them are in ruins.

silver mining areas in the world. The silver played out in the early 1950s. The mines are closed. There is a church still holding services here, but the town is nearly dead. It may be re-born, though. The town changed hands recently and the new owner hopes to make it a tourist resort. The mobile home park is growing.

The city of Marfa is in north Presidio County where U.S. 90 and U.S. 67 meet. Hunters and sail plane enthusiasts are partial to Marfa. The hunters come for the mule deer and pronghorn antelope, often visible from the highways. The soaring buffs are attracted by the winds, the climate and the wide open spaces. Several national soaring meets have been held in Marfa.

Marfa has been the county seat ever since Presidio County took its present form. But Marfa is not an old town like Presidio is. Marfa was established as a place for locomotives to take on water when the rail line that is now the Southern Pacific was first laid through here. That was in 1881. The present courthouse was built in 1886. A railroad executive's wife named the town for a character in some novel she was reading at the time.

The U.S. Army established a cavalry post here in Marfa in 1911 when revolutionary movements in Mexico were causing concern on our side of the border. The post was called Camp Marfa until 1930 when it was named Fort D. A. Russell in honor of one of the U.S. officers killed in the war with Mexico. Infantry and cavalry units trained here during World War I. The ancient and honored First Cavalry Regiment

1) The first and only courthouse built in Marfa is still in use, sitting on the square with the dignity of a mosque. The Marfa courthouse was built in 1886. 2) The old Paisano Hotel has been restored as shopping arcade, but the coffee shop is still serving coffee and meals and it is a place where you might meet some of Marfa's oldtimers.

retired its horses in a formal ceremony here in 1932 and turned itself into a motorized unit. The fort served as a training base again during World War II, and there was a camp for German prisoners of war here between 1943 and 1945. The fort was abandoned and sold after World War II.

The old Chihuahua trail used by the Indians, traders and early settlers ran along the valley of Alamito Creek between Marfa and the Rio Grande. It crossed the river about where Presidio is today and continued along the valley of the Conchos River to the Mexican town of Chihuahua. Hundreds of wagons passed this way between the 1830s and the 1880s. Mexican traders used it as a route to markets in Missouri. Texas traders used it as a route between Chihuahua and the Texas port of Indianola.

People have been reporting for years that they can see an unexplainable ghost light in the mountains outside Marfa. It is supposed to be visible at night from U.S. 90, east of Marfa and north of Paisano Pass, if you look toward the Chinati Mountains to the southwest. We are advised that a good place to stand to look for the Marfa light is at the gateway to the old abandoned air force base. The gate is really just two concrete posts on the south side of the highway. We have seen the gate. We have not seen the light.

Timber has always been scarce in this part of Texas, but the early settlers soon discovered that the mesquite here grows largely underground. They found they could dig down a few inches wherever there was a mesquite sprout and find a root

Jefferson Davis did not have a strong hold on the emotions of southerners during the Civil War when he was president of the Confederacy. But his popularity grew steadily after the war. This county is named for him. The county seat is named for him. The mountains are named for him, and the old fort was named for him. The fort was named for Davis before there was a Confederacy, though. He was secretary of war for the United States when the fort was originally established.

several inches in diameter. These mesquite roots furnished the fuel for many a pioneer's campfire.

JEFF DAVIS COUNTY

Not many people have declined the opportunity to be president of Texas A&M University. Jefferson Davis did. But Texans forgave him for it and named this county for him.

Davis was an officer in the U.S. Army when he first came to Texas with Zachary Taylor to fight in the Mexican war. He also served as a representative and a senator from Mississippi in the U.S. Congress. Davis was U.S. secretary of war in 1856 when he hatched the idea of buying camels for the army to use in West Texas. That experiment was interrupted when the southern states left the Union in 1861 and Jefferson Davis left Washington to become president of the Confederacy.

Davis was indicted for treason after the war, and he spent two years in prison. He was free and living in Mississippi when he was offered the presidency of Texas A&M in 1875. Davis had retired to write and study by that time, and he decided to continue writing and studying. Davis was not extremely popular with southerners during the war, but his popularity increased steadily after the war ended. Here in Jeff Davis County, the county seat, the fort and the mountains all are named for him. And hospitals and countless schools are, too. The legislature created this county in 1887. It was named for Davis when it was established, partly because the new county included a fort that was named for Davis in 1854. Fort Davis was established to provide protection for the settlers and wagon trains traveling toward California. Davis was

Fort Davis in the foothills of the Davis mountains was an important outpost before and after the Civil War. Most of the buildings still standing here were built after the Civil War. Some of the buildings have been restored and the old fort is open to visitors. There is a small admission fee.

secretary of war at the time. The fort was a primitive affair in the beginning. The garrison carried on intermittent warfare with the Comanches and the Apaches until the Civil War intervened. The fort was abandoned during most of the war period, and the Indians did their best to destroy it. U.S. troops returned in 1867. They built new rock and adobe buildings, and Fort Davis was a major frontier post until 1891 when it was abandoned because the Indian resistance had finally been broken. Fort Davis became a photogenic ruin.

The National Park Service took the site over in the 1960s. Some of the old buildings have been restored now, and the fort has been designated a national historic site. It looks like a movie set, but it is real and it is a reminder that our ancestors passed this way at considerable risk just one hundred years ago.

Old Fort Davis and the town that carries the same name are situated in the Davis Mountains, named for the same Jeff Davis. The town is about the same elevation as Denver. The Overland Trail came through here. It followed Limpia Canyon between Fort Davis and Fort Stockton. If interest in history and the old west continues to grow, some showman someday may round up some replicas of the Concord coaches and begin a new stage line through the Limpia Canyon. Let us hope so.

The town of Fort Davis has been the county seat of Jeff Davis County since it was established. The present courthouse

HERE LIES INDIAN EM'LY,
AN APACHE GIRL
WHOSE LOVE FOR A
YOUNG OFFICER INDUCED
HER TO GIVE WARNING OF
AN INDIAN ATTACK.
MISTAKEN FOR AN ENEMY
SHE WAS SHOT BY A
SENTRY, BUT SAVED THE
GARRISON FROM MASSACRE

Erected by the State of Texas
1936

1) *There is a state marker at Fort Davis supposedly marking the grave of an Indian girl killed by a sentry here when she tried to give warning that the Indians were planning an attack on the fort. The trouble with the story is that it is very similar to other stories about other forts, so it may not be true. 2) The Overland stagecoaches traveled through the Limpia Creek Canyon between Fort Davis and Fort Stockton. Limpia Creek begins in the Davis Mountains and flows northward toward the Pecos River.*

2

was built in 1910.

The Fort Davis Historical Society maintains the Overland Trail Museum just south of the Fort Davis National Historic Site, on the route of the Overland Trail. The museum is in a building built in the 1880s. There are several exhibits of pioneer furnishings and old photographs and records. There is an admission fee, and the museum is closed on Mondays and Tuesdays.

The Neill Museum features collections of Texas toys, bottles and dolls. It is in an old house seven blocks west of the

1) The present courthouse in Fort Davis was built in 1910. The city is about a mile high and the climate is almost universally praised. 2) An old stone hotel across from the courthouse has recently been modernized. The ceilings are high and the rooms are large and comfortable.

courthouse. The Neill Museum is open only during the summer months, and there is an admission fee here, too.

The drive out State Highway 118 from Fort Davis to State Highway 166 and then left, back around to Fort Davis, is one of the most scenic mountain drives in Texas, just as a drive. The route is about seventy-four miles. But there are at least a couple of spots on this route you will probably want to stop and visit. About six miles west of Fort Davis is the Davis Mountains State Park. It is one of the state's Class I parks and one of the best. The entrance fee is two dollars per vehicle unless you have the annual permit. The park covers nearly 2,000 acres. There are provisions for camping, and there is a comfortable lodge in this park, built by the old Civilian Conservation Corps in the 1930s. It is called Indian Lodge. It is an imitation Indian pueblo, and it is a popular place. You'd better make reservations well in advance. Write to Indian Lodge, Davis Mountains State Park, Box 786, Fort Davis, Texas 79734, or phone 915-426-3254. The rooms are priced from twelve dollars for singles to twenty-one dollars for double twins. The lodge makes a splendid base for tours of this part of the state.

The University of Texas McDonald Observatory is about twelve miles farther along Highway 118, off Spur Road 78. William Johnson McDonald made a fortune in banking in north Texas. McDonald was interested in science, and he left one million dollars in his will to establish an astronomical

1) The Overland Trail Museum in Fort Davis sits on the route the stagecoaches followed leaving Fort Davis on the way to El Paso. The building was the home of Nick Mersfelder. The Fort Davis Historical Society operates the museum. 2) The Davis Mountains State Park spreads over about two thousand acres. 3) The Indian Lodge in the park offers comfortable rooms, good food and a heated swimming pool.

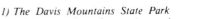

1) The Davis Mountains State Park also has a number of campsites and some trailer sites with complete hookups. 2) Visitors are welcome at the University of Texas' McDonald Observatory on top of Mount Locke, but are allowed to look through a telescope only the last Wednesday of each month by special arrangement.

observatory for the University of Texas. The school picked Mount Locke here in the Davis Mountains as the location for the observatory because of the altitude and the weather and the lack of bright artificial lights. The McDonald Observatory is one of the biggest such complexes in the world now. There are tours for the public every day. But the only time that visitors are allowed to look through the telescopes is on the last Wednesday of each month. Arrangements have to be made in advance through the observatory office, Fort Davis, Texas 79734. You should include a self-addressed, stamped envelope for the reply.

There is an experiment in grape culture going on at the base of Blue Mountain, seven miles west of Fort Davis on State Highway 166. Gretchen Glasscock of San Antonio is growing vinfera grapes in a vineyard covering about forty-seven acres here. She says she is convinced the climate is comparable to

1) The Glasscock Vineyard is experimenting with wine grapes on the lower slope of Blue Mountain southwest of Fort Davis. 2) Nearby is Skillman Grove, where the Bloys religious camp meetings have been held every summer since 1889. 3) Lelia Doris Kelley, the postmaster for Valentine, will re-mail valentines with the Valentine postmark.

that in the Napa Valley region of California, so she is trying to prove that growing wine grapes in the Davis Mountains makes sense, and money. Ms. Glasscock says she will build a winery, and she is trying to encourage other landowners in the mountains to plant wine grapes.

Today's major highways miss the main part of Jeff Davis County. Interstate 10 cuts across the northern tip of the county, and U.S. 90 cuts across the southwestern corner. U.S. 90 and the Southern Pacific tracks both pass through a little settlement called Valentine. The accepted story is that the town was named Valentine because the Southern Pacific line reached this point on Saint Valentine's Day in 1882. The post office here gets a big rush every February. Tourists stop at the

The Balmorhea State Park is built around the old San Solomon Springs, discovered by the early Spanish explorers and known to the Indians before that. Water flows out of the ground here at the rate of twenty million gallons a day. Much of it is used to irrigate surrounding farms but there is plenty left to keep the two-acre swimming pool in the park filled with clean circulating spring water.

post office in Valentine to mail valentine cards and gifts so they will have the Valentine post mark. And the postmaster is willing to re-mail valentines for anybody, anywhere. The postmaster is Lelia Doris Kelley. If you have valentines you want sent out with the Valentine post mark, you should address and stamp them and put them in an envelope addressed to Postmaster, Valentine, Texas 79854. Ms. Kelley will do the rest.

REEVES COUNTY

Transcontinental travelers have been passing this way since the middle 1850s. The Butterfield Overland Trail came through here, and two interstate highways cross the county today. Interstate 20 from Dallas joins and merges with Interstate 10 from Houston at the western edge of Reeves County.

Interstate 20 passes by the county seat at Pecos. Interstate 10 passes by Balmorhea. There is a prolific spring at Balmorhea that was known to the earliest Spanish adventurers and to the Indians before them. San Solomon Springs has been flowing at the rate of 20 million gallons a day for as long as its history has been recorded.

The water is used to irrigate farmlands in Balmorhea,

The present courthouse in Pecos was built in 1937. The county was named for George R. Reeves. He was a colonel in the Confederate army and he was speaker of the Texas House. He died shortly before this county was created and named for him.

Saragosa and Toyahvale. And a huge swimming pool has been built around the spring. The pool covers two acres. Parts of it are thirty feet deep. It is clear and full of fish and very popular with bathers, skin divers and scuba divers. It is about the last thing you would expect to find in this part of the West Texas desert. The state acquired the land around the spring in 1934 and turned it into a park. It is known as the Balmorhea State Recreation Area and you get to it by taking the Farm Road 2903 exit from Interstate 10, traveling two miles south to Balmorhea and then taking U.S. 290 to Toyahvale. The Balmorhea Recreation Area has provisions for camping and a lodge called San Solomon Springs Courts. The fee for admission to the park is two dollars per vehicle. There are additional charges for admission to the pool and for lodging or campsites. For reservations at San Solomon Springs Courts, write to Balmorhea State Recreation Area, Box 15, Toyahvale, Texas 79786, or phone 915-375-2370.

The natural advantages of this location are such that it is surprising there was no town here until 1906 when three real estate promoters named Balcom, Morrow and Rhea laid one out and gave it a name they made up by combining their names.

Reeves County was created by the legislature in 1883 from part of Pecos County. The town of Pecos has been the county

1) Pecos cantaloupes are widely regarded as the tastiest in the world. 2) The vines grow in the hot west Texas sun with little rain, but with ample irrigation.

seat of Reeves County since the county was created. The town grew out of a settlement that began originally on the east bank of the Pecos River. Sometime around 1881, when the Texas & Pacific Railroad came through, the settlement moved to the west bank of the river. Some question arose about the title to the land on the west bank, and a landowner named George Knight offered the T&P enough land for a depot and several extra city blocks a little farther west. The railroad accepted the offer and built its station on Knight's land. The community of Pecos moved to the railroad station, and it has been in this location ever since. The present courthouse was built in 1937.

The county has substantial income from oil and gas. Farming and ranching are also important here, and the cantaloupes grown here are famous all over the country. They are at their best in the months of July and August.

Pecos claims to have been the site of the very first rodeo. There seems to be some doubt whether it was called a rodeo then. But cowboys from the Hashknife Ranch, the 101, the Mill Iron and several other ranches got together here in Pecos in 1883 to stage some contests, and that event got recorded as the original rodeo. The people of Pecos have been putting on a rodeo regularly every year since 1929. It is held usually around the Fourth of July. The first cowgirls' barrel race was

1) *The West of the Pecos Museum occupies the entire Orient Hotel building and the restored saloon next door. The Orient, in Pecos, was one of the finest hotels in this part of the state in its heyday. The railroad depot was very close by, but the Orient maintained a big bus, pulled by a team of white horses. And that bus met every train to ferry the passengers and their luggage to the hotel. 2) One of the noted gunfighters of the early days is buried on the museum grounds outside the old hotel and saloon. There were at least two killings in the saloon here, but Clay Allison was not one of the victims. This gunfighter was killed in an accident. There is also a replica of Judge Roy Bean's courthouse on the museum grounds.*

staged at the Pecos Rodeo in 1945.

There is a museum here in the old Orient Hotel building at First and Cedar streets (U.S. 285). The museum occupies the saloon and most of the old hotel. Exhibits include period furnishings, rock and mineral collections and historical items. The museum is open all day, Mondays through Saturdays, and on Sunday afternoons from two to four. There is a small admission charge. A gunman named Barney Riggs shot two members of the Jim Miller gang to death in the Orient Hotel Saloon in 1896, and there is a nick in the wall supposedly caused by a stray bullet fired during that encounter.

Another gunfighter of note in old Pecos was Clay Allison. They called him the gentleman gunfighter for reasons that are not entirely clear. Allison brought his wife and two daughters to Pecos in 1886. He supposedly survived showdowns with Bat Masterson and Wyatt Earp only to be crushed to death by

1

1) *The oldest town in Reeves county is almost a ghost town today. Toyah is about fifteen miles southwest of Pecos and it was a substantial town for a few years after the Texas & Pacific railroad built its line through here. The railroad had a big shop here. There were plenty of jobs and enough business to justify a Harvey House this size. 2) The shops and the Harvey House are gone now. And most of the buildings left on the main street are abandoned.*

2

a freight wagon he was driving from Pecos to his ranch on the Pecos River, shortly after he settled here.

The oldest settlement in Reeves County is Toyah. This town is just off Interstate 20, about fifteen miles west of Pecos. It has been in a decline for a number of years. But Toyah was a major freight division point on the T&P railroad in the early days. There were shops and plenty of railroad jobs here then. Toyah's decline began when the railroad changed to diesels and consolidated its shops at Big Spring.

There was some excitement here in Toyah on September 6, 1928. Amelia Earhart made a forced landing. Alton Hughes says in his book *Pecos* that she had taken on some bad gasoline during a re-fueling stop at Pecos a short time earlier and her engine quit. The famous flyer turned her plane over to a local mechanic and spent three or four days being enter-

1) Some of the stagecoaches and wagon trains traveling across west Texas toward California in the 1850s and 1870s crossed the Pecos River at one place and some at another. There were three main crossings. This was the Emigrant Crossing, southeast of the present city of Pecos. It is on private property. You can wade across the Pecos here, now, but there was much more water here in the stagecoach days. A dam has been built upstream since then. 2) The dam that brought the Pecos River under control is the Red Bluff Dam near Orla at the northern end of Pecos county near the New Mexico line. The lake created by the dam now covers what was known as Pope's Crossing.

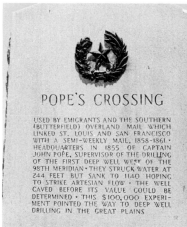

POPE'S CROSSING

USED BY EMIGRANTS AND THE SOUTHERN (BUTTERFIELD) OVERLAND MAIL WHICH LINKED ST. LOUIS AND SAN FRANCISCO WITH A SEMI-WEEKLY MAIL, 1858-1861 • HEADQUARTERS IN 1855 OF CAPTAIN JOHN POPE, SUPERVISOR OF THE DRILLING OF THE FIRST DEEP WELL WEST OF THE 98TH MERIDIAN • THEY STRUCK WATER AT 244 FEET BUT SANK TO 1140 HOPING TO STRIKE ARTESIAN FLOW • THE WELL CAVED BEFORE ITS VALUE COULD BE DETERMINED • THIS $100,000 EXPERIMENT POINTED THE WAY TO DEEP WELL DRILLING IN THE GREAT PLAINS

2

tained and fussed over in Pecos. She was quoted as saying she had the best time in Pecos that she'd ever had in her life.

Two of the old river crossing points of the Butterfield Overland days were in what is now Reeves County.

There is a state marker in the town of Pecos, at U.S. 285 and First Street, recalling that Emigrant Crossing was nearby. Historian Alton Hughes says it was actually about twenty miles southeast of Pecos, below the junction of Toyah Creek and the Pecos River.

The stages and the wagon trains heading westward usually traveled along either the east or west bank of the Pecos River from Emigrant Crossing to Pope's Crossing near the New Mexico border. The actual site of Pope's Crossing, where the trail turned due west toward Pine Springs and El Paso, is probably beneath the waters of Red Bluff Reservoir now. But there is a state marker on U.S. 285, six miles northwest of the

1) Van Horn Wells was the site of a stage station on the line from San Antonio to San Diego. The station was attacked by Indians one night in 1879. There is nothing left but the well itself, now, about a half mile off U.S. 90. 2) The well and the town were named for army officer James Judson Van Horn. He was in command at the stage station in 1859 and 1860.

town of Orla. The water in Red Bluff Reservoir is fairly salty and the State Parks and Wildlife Department has been stocking the lake experimentally with redfish and other saltwater species.

CULBERSON COUNTY

The last battles between the Apaches and the white settlers were fought here in Culberson County just a hundred years ago. There was no Culberson County at the time. This area was part of El Paso County then. The stage line from San Antonio to San Diego passed through the southern end of what is now Culberson County. And the Butterfield Overland stage line skirted across the northern end of the present county. The Butterfield Overland had a way station near where the settlement of Pine Springs is today. The line from San Antonio to San Diego had a station at Van Horn Wells close to the present settlement of Lobo. The station at Van Horn Wells was an adobe building, built like a fort. There were four men on duty at the station when the Apaches attacked the place one night in 1879. Culberson County historian Rosa Lee Wylie says, in her *History of Van Horn and Culberson County,* that the Indians set fire to the hay in the corral and they and the four men inside the station then exchanged shots throughout the night. There were thirty Indians by this account. Several of them were killed during the night, and the four white men were able to slip safely

1) Van Horn was named for a Union officer, but Culberson County was named for Confederate officer, David B. Culberson. 2) Van Horn has been the county seat for Culberson County since the county was created in 1912. The courthouse is not an old one. It was built in 1964. 3) The old Clark Hotel was built in 1901 in the heyday of the passenger train era and is the oldest permanent building in Van Horn.

away from the ruined stage station the next morning. There is an historical marker at Van Horn Wells, twelve miles south of Van Horn on U.S. 90. Mrs. Wylie says the last battle between Indians and whites in this part of the world was fought in Victoria Canyon in the Diablo Mountains twenty-five miles north of Van Horn in 1881. Rangers killed several Apaches and captured a few others after the Indians ambushed a small party of settlers.

Culberson County has the highest mountain peak in Texas. The low areas here are 3,000 feet above sea level. The climate is like some other state. There is some oil and gas. There is a little mining. There are some irrigated farms, but the principal occupations here are ranching and entertaining tourists.

1) *The Van Horn State Bank does its business in a building that was built originally in the 1920s as a hotel. This was the El Capitan. It was the finest stopping place in Van Horn in the twenties and early thirties.* 2) *Texas has only about half a dozen mountains taller than eight thousand feet and more than half of them are here. The most famous and most imposing and most photographed is El Capitan.* 3) *El Capitan's twin, Guadalupe Peak, is actually taller. Guadalupe is 8721 feet high, the highest mountain in the state.*

2

3

Interstate Highway 10 crosses the lower part of Culberson County, and it meets U.S. Highway 90 at Van Horn. The town is named for Colonel J. J. Van Horn of the U.S. Army. He was in command of the troops stationed here to protect the settlers and travelers in 1859. Van Horn became the county seat when Culberson County was formed from part of El Paso County in 1912.

The county was named for David Browning Culberson. He came to Texas from Alabama to practice law. He fought in the Civil War with the Eighteenth Texas Infantry and became a lieutenant colonel. Culberson served in the Texas legislature after the war, and he was elected to ten consecutive terms in the U.S. House of Representatives. He died in 1900, twelve years before Culberson County was created.

The present courthouse in Van Horn was built in 1964.

1) *The Guadalupe Mountains are wrapped around a unique valley called McKittrick Canyon. There are plants and trees here that do not grow anywhere else in Texas. The canyon is the chief attraction of the Guadalupe Mountains National Park. It is a wilderness and only hikers can see most of it. 2) The park includes the ruins of the old stage station the Butterfield Line called The Pinery. The ruins are just inside the park, about where U.S. 180 crosses Pine Springs Canyon.*

The Culberson County Historical Museum behind the courthouse at Fourth and Austin streets features Indian artifacts and items used by the early white settlers here. The museum is housed in the old Honeycutt House.

The Hazel Mines north of Van Horn produced silver for a number of years after they were discovered in 1856. Iron and coal, mica and talc have been mined in Culberson County at various times, too.

Serious development of the resources and serious settlement of Culberson County began when the Texas & Pacific Railroad came through in 1882. The T&P provided side tours to Carlsbad Caverns for many years by detaching a passenger car or two here at Van Horn and providing a bus to take the passengers to the caverns and back. The side trip took all day.

El Capitan Hotel was the showplace here in the twenties and early thirties. It was closed for a number of years. Now

Claude B. Hudspeth probably had something personally to do with getting this county named in his honor. He was serving in the legislature when the legislature decided to separate this area from El Paso County and make it a separate county. Hudspeth later served several terms in the U.S. Congress.

it's been remodeled to house a bank. The hotel was named for one of the county's most conspicuous landmarks. El Capitan and Guadalupe are the two tallest peaks in the Guadalupe Mountains in the northwest corner of Culberson County. The Guadalupe Mountains National Park here includes the unique McKittrick Canyon.

The National Park Service acquired a total of more than 77,000 acres here after geologist Wallace Pratt donated the first 6,000 acres. Pratt's summer home is still here in the park and the ruins of an early stage stop are here, too. This was the site of The Pinery station on the Butterfield Overland run from St. Louis to San Francisco. But there is nothing left of the stage stand except some fragments of stone work and a marker.

The Guadalupe Mountains National Park is for determined outdoors people. Only primitive camping is allowed. Overnight campers must obtain special permits. There are no roads to the scenic interior of this park and only backpackers can see it. The information station is at Pine Springs on U.S. 62-180.

HUDSPETH COUNTY

Hudspeth County was formed in 1917 from part of what had been El Paso County. Its southern boundary is the Mexican border and its northern boundary is the New Mexico state line. Hudspeth County has two time zones. The boun-

1) There is a very large deposit of salt in the northeastern corner of Hudspeth County, at the base of Guadalupe Peak. 2) This stone marker on Highway 180, near the town of Salt Flat recalls the fighting that broke out here when the property owners declared that the salt was theirs. 3) The only adobe courthouse still in use in Texas is the Hudspeth County Courthouse at Sierra Blanca, built in 1919.

dary line between the central time zone and the mountain time zone actually is the eastern boundary of Hudspeth County, so the entire county officially is in the mountain time zone. But the railroads and the federal offices here keep central time. The rest of the county keeps mountain time.

Hudspeth County was named for a native of Medina County. Claude Benton Hudspeth was a rancher, a peace officer and a newspaper editor before he went into politics. Hudspeth served in the Texas legislature and he was a member of Congress for twelve years.

The western part of the Guadalupe Mountains National Park extends into the northeastern corner of Hudspeth County, but the park entrance is in Culberson County.

225

1) The oldest protestant church in Hudspeth County is the First Methodist in Sierra Blanca. It was built in 1909 and it also has been used as a school. 2) There were two border forts in what is now Hudspeth County in the early days. The army established Fort Quitman in 1858 to protect settlers and discourage the Indians from raiding into Mexico. Fort Quitman was abandoned in 1877 and nothing is left of it. A businessman has built an adobe scale model of the old fort at Tommystown, on I-10 a few miles east of McNary, but it is not often open.

2

There is a large salt deposit at the western base of Guadalupe Peak here in the northeast corner of Hudspeth County. This salt provoked some bitter fighting that came to be called the Salt War. It happened after the Civil War. All mineral deposits in Texas, up until that time, had been considered the property of the state. It was an arrangement passed down by the Spanish and the Mexicans. People here had been accustomed to helping themselves to the salt for as long as they could remember. The Republicans brought in the concept of private mineral rights when they gained control of the state government during the so-called reconstruction. The adherents of these two concepts fought several gun battles during the late 1860s and early 1870s. There were several people killed on both sides. The concept of private mineral rights eventually prevailed, to the great benefit of subsequent generations of royalty owners and oil developers.

The county seat of Hudspeth County is the town of Sierra Blanca on Interstate Highway 10. The town was established in 1881 when the Texas & Pacific and the Southern Pacific

Fort Hancock was established in 1882. It was abandoned in 1890 and there is nothing left except this marker, built from some of the ruins of the old fort. The marker is on I-10 at the eastern edge of the town of Fort Hancock.

railroads met here. The town takes its name from a mountain just outside town. Sierra Blanca is Spanish for white mountain. The town never has grown very much. The population hovers under a thousand.

There is little mineral production. The principal occupations are ranching and farming.

Sierra Blanca is the only county seat in Texas still using an adobe building for a courthouse. It is listed in the *National Register of Historic Places.* The courthouse is on Millican Street. It was built in 1919.

Sierra Blanca is on the route the old stage line from San Antonio to San Diego followed before the railroads came. The old Indian Hot Springs resort is still operating on the border south of Sierra Blanca. There is a hotel and a dining room and not much else, but people still come here for the hot baths. Indian Hot Springs is on Ranch Road 1111, beside the Rio Grande.

Interstate 10 runs along the Rio Grande for most of the distance from Sierra Blanca to the western county line. And there were two old forts on this route.

The peace treaty that ended the war between the United States and Mexico in 1848 settled the southern boundary of Texas and conveyed New Mexico and a lot more territory to the United States. The United States paid Mexico fifteen million dollars in this settlement and also accepted responsibility for discouraging Indian attacks across the Rio Grande. The U.S. Army established a number of forts along the river after that agreement was signed. Fort Quitman was established in 1858. It was abandoned in 1877, but there is a

American explorer Zebulon Pike made a visit to this corner of the world in 1807. The U.S. had just bought the Louisiana Territory from France. Pike was sent out in command of a small party to explore the new territory and to see what he could learn about the Spanish territory to the west, also. The explorer discovered Pike's Peak and then he came on south to the Rio Grande. He bumped into some Spaniards and he and his party were taken into custody. They were detained until they convinced the Spanish authorities they meant no harm. Then they were escorted to the eastern border and turned over to American authorities in Louisiana. Pike wrote a book about it.

replica on Interstate 10 about ten miles east of the town of McNary. Some early weapons, implements and Indian artifacts are on display here. There is a charge for admission, but the place is not often open.

Fort Hancock is a few miles farther west on Interstate 10. This little town grew up around a military outpost that was established in 1882 and abandoned in 1890. Only ruins remain at the site of old Fort Hancock, named for General Winfield Scott Hancock.

EL PASO COUNTY

Some of the oldest settlements in Texas are scattered along Interstate Highway 10 between the Hudspeth County line and the city of El Paso.

The early Spanish explorers were conditioned by their experiences in Mexico and Peru to look for rich cities and gold mines in the areas they claimed. Rumors that the seven cities of Cibola and the city of Quivira were full of treasures caused Viceroy Antonio de Mendoza to send his friend Francisco Vasquez de Coronado on an expedition into what is now New Mexico and the Texas panhandle in 1541 and 1542. Coronado never found any treasure. But he found Indian cities in New Mexico. And the Spanish missionaries decided the Indians had to be converted. A party of colonists, priests and soldiers moved to New Mexico in the 1590s. By this time the travelers between Mexico and New Mexico were crossing the Rio Grande fairly regularly at a place they called El Paso del Norte. The spot became a campground for the Spanish caravans and for the Indians, too. A primitive mission was

1) There is a steak house outside Fabens in the eastern end of El Paso County that does things a little differently. The Cattleman's Steakhouse on the Indian Cliffs Ranch serves steak dinners in the restaurant and also offers an overnight campout. 2) If you make reservations ahead of time, you can ride a modernized covered wagon to a remote part of the ranch and have your steak dinner under the stars. The ranch hands set up an overnight camp and serve a cowboy breakfast before they drive the guests back to the steakhouse the next morning.

1

2

established here in 1659 to minister to the Manso and Suma Indians. A permanent church was finished in 1668. It was on the south side of the river in what is now the city of Juárez. Part of that structure is incorporated in the old cathedral still standing in Juárez. About a thousand people were living around the pass by 1670. The population of the area was more than doubled suddenly in 1680 because the Indians in Santa Fe and the other settlements in New Mexico revolted. The frightened Spanish settlers moved south to the pass.

Parts of the Rio Grande valley here have been under cultivation for more than three hundred years. U.S. explorer Zebulon Pike was here briefly in 1807 as a prisoner of the Spanish. He reported seeing finely cultivated vineyards and fields of wheat and other grains. Pike was on the expedition during which he discovered Pike's Peak in Colorado. The Spanish were suspicious of Yankees exploring their territory. They detained him for a while and then escorted him out of Texas by way of Nacogdoches.

1

1) The village of San Elizario is more than two hundred years old and this building is older than the town. It is usually referred to as the Viceroy's Palace and was probably built about 1683. 2) It is not open very often but there is a little museum in the old jail building in San Elizario.

2

One of the state's more unusual eating places is off Interstate Highway 10 in eastern El Paso County. The Cattleman's Steakhouse at Fabens is a restaurant with a view and a whole lot more. The Cattleman's offers steak dinners in the restaurant, or an overnight campout, with a chuckwagon dinner and breakfast. There are horses and wagons to carry adventurous diners to the campsite called Fort Misery in a remote section of the Indian Cliffs Ranch. Reservations should be made in advance with the Indian Cliffs Ranch, Box 1056, Fabens, 79839 or 915-764-2284.

San Elizario is not one of the older towns in this section of the Rio Grande valley. San Elizario was established at this site in 1772 when the Spanish moved a presidio here that originally had been established on the south side of the river. The presidio was later moved on to another location, but San Elizario continued to prosper for a number of years. The town was made the county seat when the Texas legislature created El Paso County in 1850. The county government later moved to Ysleta and then to El Paso, and San Elizario began

2

1

3

1) The Spanish built a mission at Socorro in 1682. It was destroyed by a flood in 1829 and rebuilt in 1840. 2) One of the settlements claiming to be the oldest in Texas is Ysleta. Missionaries and a band of friendly Tigua Indians came here and built a mission in 1682. 3) The Tigua Indians are still here and still friendly. They live in adobe pueblos adjacent to the mission and visitors are welcome.

to decline. One of the buildings here in San Elizario may be the oldest dwelling in Texas. It is referred to as the Viceroy's Palace, and it is said to have been built in 1683. The building is now being restored.

The original presidio chapel built here in 1773 was destroyed after the presidio was moved. A new chapel was built in 1877, and it is still standing here on old U.S. 80 in San Elizario. It is listed in the *National Register of Historic Places.* There is a museum in the old jail building in San Elizario featuring articles from the Indian and colonial days. The museum is open only weekend afternoons and by special arrangement. There is a small fee. The register also lists the old mission in the much older town of Socorro, a few miles farther up the valley. The Mission Socorro was established in 1682 during the building boom that followed the arrival of the refugees from the Indian uprising in New Mexico. The original mission and the town were largely destroyed by a flood in 1829. The mission now standing at Farm Road 258 and Moon Road in Socorro was rebuilt in 1840.

1

1) El Paso is the biggest city on the U.S. side of the Mexican border with a population nearing four hundred thousand. El Paso is prosperous, cosmopolitan and livable. The climate is mild, dry and pleasant. 2) Wagon trains and stagecoaches passed this way when the west was young. The Overland Mail line had a station occupying a whole city block here in the 1850s. The site is now downtown El Paso.

2

The settlement of Ysleta is a very short distance farther up the valley and within the present city limits of El Paso. Ysleta claims to be the oldest town in Texas. The mission here is supposed to be the oldest one within the present boundaries of Texas. It was established after the Indian uprising in New Mexico in 1682, by Spanish missionaries and a band of Tigua Indians. The mission has been called by several names, but the name usually used today is Corpus Christi de la Isleta. It is also listed in the *National Register of Historic Places,* but the building is not the original one. The mission now standing on old U.S. 90 here was first built on this site in 1744 and then rebuilt in 1907 after a fire destroyed most of it.

The Tigua Indians have survived, and they have preserved

1) There is a free bridge across the Rio Grande in the Chamizal area. This is the Bridge of the Americas, built to celebrate the peaceful resolution of an old dispute between Mexico and the United States. 2) The county seat in El Paso County moved back and forth between San Elizario and Ysleta a couple of times before it was moved permanently to the city of El Paso in 1883. The courthouse is incorporated in the new El Paso City-County Building.

2

substantial parts of their culture. They live in adobe pueblos around the old mission church. They conduct tours of their picturesque reservation, and they make and sell pottery, blankets, jewelry, and some very tasty Indian foods.

If you are approaching Ysleta from Interstate 10, you take the exit marked Avenue of the Americas. There is a fee for the tours of the Tigua Reservation. They are offered daily during the summer months. They are conducted only on weekends during the fall and winter.

The city of El Paso is a surprise to many visitors. The early settlements at the Pass of the North were on the other side of the river, where Juárez is today. The city that became El Paso grew out of a settlement established in 1827 by Juan María Ponce de León. A man named Franklin Coons bought de León out in about 1848. He named the settlement Franklin, got himself made postmaster and started doing a little trading with the wagon trains passing through on the way to California. The arrangement surely would have made him very rich. The land was the land that is now downtown El Paso. But Franklin Coons moved away after a couple of years, without

1) The Chamizal Treaty Memorial on the Texas side is a theater for performing arts. 2) In the new Pronaf area in Juárez there is a large Centro Artesanal operated by the Mexican government selling handmade Mexican products, but some shoppers find the old Mercado Juárez downtown more entertaining. 3) The city of Juárez was originally called Paso del Norte. The name was changed in 1888 to honor the patriot Benito Juárez. He led the revolution that ended the rule and the life of the foreign emperor Maximilian in 1867.

ever paying de León the full price for the land. William T. Smith bought the property in 1854. The Butterfield Overland Mail established a stage station at the corner of El Paso Street and Overland in 1858. The station was torn down a long time ago. The name of the settlement was changed to El Paso in 1859. The Mexican town across the river continued to be called Paso del Norte until 1888 when the name was changed to Juárez to honor Benito Juárez.

El Paso is one of the state's major cities. It is also the biggest city on the U.S. side of the Mexican border. And Juárez, on the other side of the toll bridge, is the biggest border city in Mexico. The climate is mild and sunny. The scenery is dif-

Presidents of the United States and Mexico have met at various border points at various times since William Howard Taft and Porfirio Diaz started the custom in 1909. Their meeting here in Juárez was to dedicate the monument to Benito Juárez.

ferent. The atmosphere is cosmopolitan. The attractions are varied. The Sun Carnival during the last week in December includes the Sun Bowl football game in the stadium at 306 North Mesa. There is horse racing and greyhound racing, and there are bullfights and Charro rodeos in the arena across the river in Juárez. (See index for information about crossing the border.)

The El Paso County Courthouse is included in the new City-County Building at Kansas and San Antonio streets.

The first meeting between a president of the United States and a president of Mexico took place here at the Juárez Customshouse in 1909. Our President William Howard Taft met with Mexico's Porfirio Diaz just a year before Francisco Madero and Pancho Villa mounted the revolution that ended Diaz' long term as president. The citizens of El Paso were interested spectators when Villa's rebels captured the city of Juárez from Diaz' troops in 1911. Villa later lived in El Paso for several months as an exile and became a familiar figure at the Elite Confectionary where, C. L. Sonnichsen says in his *Pass of the North,* the famous revolutionary liked to eat ice cream. Villa's later raids on both sides of the border provoked President Woodrow Wilson into sending General John J. Pershing and several thousand U.S. soldiers into northern Mexico in 1916.

One of the early Anglo settlers in this area was James Wiley Magoffin. He was a trader in Mexico before the Texas

1) Pancho Villa was a familiar figure in Juárez and El Paso, too. Villa supported Francisco Madero's revolution against the Díaz government in 1910 and Villa and his followers captured the city of Juárez in 1911. A little later, he lived in El Paso, as an exile, for a little while. 2) The El Paso Museum of Art has a collection of pre-Columbian art and some paintings from the Kress art collection on permanent display. The museum is near downtown at 1211 Montana and it is free.

EL PASO MUSEUM OF ART

Revolution and he was a special agent for the U.S. Army during the war between the United States and Mexico. The United States government paid Magoffin thirty thousand dollars at the end of the war, and he invested the money in real estate. He established a trading post and village near the Rio Grande and called it Magoffinsville. The site is now within the city limits of El Paso at Magoffin and Octavia streets. And it is now the property of the State Department of Parks and Wildlife. The imposing home James Magoffin

1

1) The University of Texas at El Paso is off Interstate 10 west of downtown El Paso. The El Paso Centennial Museum on the U.T.E.P. campus has exhibits tracing the history of the area with emphasis on geology and archaeology. The campus is at the base of Franklin Mountain. 2) The mountainside site inspired the design of some of the buildings on the U.T.E.P. campus. They are designed to resemble the monasteries in Tibet. The Sun Bowl is also on this campus.

2

built here was destroyed by a flood in 1868. Magoffin's son, Joseph, rebuilt the house in 1875, and the family donated it to the state in 1965. The parks department is doing some restoration work now and plans to have the Magoffin place open to visitors as a state historic site by the summer of 1980. There will be a fee for tours of the Magoffin place.

The Chamizal National Memorial Museum is in a theater for the performing arts established to commemorate the peaceful resolution of a boundary dispute between the United States and Mexico in 1963. The address is 800 South Marcial. There is no charge for admission to the museum. The international bridge here is also free.

The El Paso Cavalry Museum at Interstate 10 and Loop 375 has mementos and pictures tracing the history of the southwest. It is free, and it is open Sunday afternoons and all day weekdays, except Monday.

The El Paso Museum of Art at 1211 Montana Avenue has

1) *An aerial tramway in northwest El Paso carries sightseers to the top of Ranger Peak. 2) The U.S. Army established a fort here at El Paso in 1848. The fort is named for William W. S. Bliss. He was a member of Zachary Taylor's staff during the war with Mexico. The fort was surrendered to the Confederates in 1861 but Union troops re-took it in 1862 and remained in control through the remainder of the Civil War.*

paintings from the Kress collection of European and American art on permanent display. The museum also has a collection of pre-Columbian art. It is open weekdays, except Mondays, and on Sunday afternoons. There is no charge for admission.

The El Paso Centennial Museum features displays covering the geology, archaeology and historical development of the El Paso area. The Centennial Museum is on the lower slope of the Franklin Mountains on the campus of the University of Texas at El Paso. This is the school that earlier was called the Texas School of Mines and Metallurgy. It is distinguished for, among other things, several buildings designed to look like monasteries in Tibet. The museum is on University Avenue at Wiggins Road.

The Sierra de Cristo Rey rises above El Paso at about the spot where the boundaries of Texas, New Mexico and Mexico meet. Near the summit of the mountain is a white limestone statue of Christ on the cross. Pilgrims climb four miles up the trail to the statue on the last Sunday of October to observe the feast day of Christ the King.

You can get a great view of El Paso and the surrounding countryside from the top of Ranger Peak. There is an aerial tramway operating every day during the summer months. It operates every day except Tuesday and Wednesday during the winter. You catch the tram at McKinley and Piedras. The fare is $1.50 for adults and 75¢ for children under twelve.

Fort Bliss now spreads over more than one million acres. It is bigger than the state of Rhode Island. The fort is now the army's Air Defense Training Center and it is open to visitors. There are displays of old and new military hardware and replicas of the four original Fort Bliss buildings at the Fort Bliss Replica Museum off U.S. 54 in northeast El Paso. There is no admission charge here and the museum is open every day.

You can get some high altitude views here from your own car by taking the scenic drive across the southern flank of Mount Franklin. You can get onto this drive from Richmond Street on the east, or from Rim Road on the west. And the views from Loop 375 between Interstate 10 and U.S. 54, north of the city, are worth seeing, too.

El Paso County is a major center of manufacturing and retailing. Many large U.S. corporations have plants on the border here to take advantage of cheaper labor. Government payrolls are a big factor in the economy, too. Fort Bliss spreads over more than a quarter of the county and extends into New Mexico.

Fort Bliss was established in 1848 at the end of the Mexican War. It was originally called the Post of El Paso, and the original site was about where Main and Santa Fe streets meet in the present city of El Paso. The fort moved in 1854 to a site on James Magoffin's ranch, and the name was changed to Fort Bliss in honor of Colonel William W. S. Bliss. He had been Zachary Taylor's adjutant during the Mexican War. The site on Magoffin's ranch was subject to flooding, so the fort was moved again after the Civil War and then moved again in 1890. It was a base for the expedition against Pancho Villa in 1916. It has been an infantry base and a cavalry base at different times, and it is now the largest air defense training center in the western world.

There is a museum on the grounds of Fort Bliss. It is a replica of the original fort. There are four buildings with exhibits tracing the development of weapons and military equipment. One of the exhibits is a relief map showing the old stage lines and wagon trails.

Travelers have been camping at Hueco Tanks for thousands of years. This is a large rock formation with many holes and natural basins which catch and hold rainwater so this has been a reliable watering hole since the early days. The Butterfield stage stopped here, as did the Indians for generations before that.

There is a strange rock formation about thirty miles east of El Paso called Hueco Tanks. Natural rock basins here catch and hold rainwater, so this spot has been a rest stop for travelers for thousands of years. The Butterfield Overland had a station here for a time. The rock formations include a number of shelters and overhangs and generations of Indians drew pictures here.

A party of Apaches was massacred by Mexican troops here about 1840. The boundary between Texas and Mexico had not yet been settled and Mexico still claimed the area. The Apaches so terrorized the Mexican settlers that Mexican officials had a standing offer of one hundred pesos for each Apache scalp. A few adventurers were able to make a living for a time in the 1840s by tracking down, killing and scalping Apaches. But the Apaches were not easy to discourage. Those trapped here at Hueco Tanks had just made a raid on one of the Mexican settlements to the south. C. L. Sonnichsen quotes a Captain John Pope as reporting more than one hundred Indians killed in the engagement here.

The Hueco Tanks area is now a state park. There is an admission fee of two dollars per vehicle and there are provisions for camping. You can arrange reservations by writing to Hueco Tanks State Historic Site, Box 26502, Ranchland Station, El Paso, 79926, or by phoning 915-859-4100. The entrance to this park is from Ranch Road 2775, off U.S. 62-180.

You are now approximately 800 miles from the eastern boundary of Texas.

Native Plants

1

1) Travelers visiting this part of west Texas for the first time will be seeing some desert plants they may not recognize. Some of these, most likely to be seen from the road are the low yucca known as Spanish Dagger. 2) Also common throughout this area is the taller yucca known as Giant Dagger. These plants are widely used in landscaping in other areas, but this is their native land. 3) The Thompson Yucca resembles the giant dagger, but the spines are skinnier.

2

3

1

1) *The sotol grows close to the ground with spines, or leaves, thinner than the yucca. The early Pecos River people used the fibers of the sotol to make baskets and mats and they cooked and ate the hearts of these plants. 2) The lechuguilla is a member of the agave family and this plant was very useful to the early Indians, too. The fibers are extremely strong and tough and the Mexicans still sometimes make ropes from them. 3) The cholla is also called the walking stick cactus. This plant makes a small tree and the limbs are strong enough to be used as walking canes. The cholla puts out a purple bloom in the spring.*

2

3

1) The century plant is the most generally familiar member of the agave family. How useful this plant is may be open to some question. It is the plant used in the manufacture of tequila, mescal and pulque. The stalk behind this plant is part of a different plant. But the century plants, and other agaves, do put up stalks after they reach a certain age. The stalk blooms and the plant then dies, but it usually has put out several new plants from the base by that time. They usually bloom at somewhere between eight and twenty years of age. 2) The ocotillo is more shrub than cactus. The ocotillo puts out long spindly limbs from the base. The limbs are covered with small green leaves and brilliant red blooms form at the ends of the limbs in the spring. The limbs of the ocotillo can reach a height of 25 feet. 3) The desert willow is one of the plants the Texas Department of Highways and Public Transportation is planting along the roads and highways in this part of the state.

1

1) The creosote bush, or greasewood, grows all over this part of Texas. The Indians and the pioneers used this plant for various medicinal purposes. It has a smell vaguely like that of creosote. 2) The Ceniza is very widely and mistakenly referred to as purple sage. This small shrub has foliage that is more gray than green and it puts out small purple blooms after a rain. It is used in landscaping all over the southwest. 3) The one cactus everybody knows is the prickly pear. Cows will eat the leaves if the needles are burned off and many people enjoy the jelly some Texas housewives make from the fruit of the prickly pear.

2

3

Index

Photo Credits:

All of the photos for this book, with the exception of those listed below, were made by Gary James, Bill Springer, Ray Miller, Mark Williams, John Treadgold and Bob Brandon.

The first number indicates the page, the second number indicates the number of the picture on that page.

Aultman Collection — El Paso Library: 235
Dept. of Parks and Wildlife: 192-2
Tom Farris: 123-1
Haley's Trading Post: 191-2
Houston Public Library: 4, 5, 15-1, 24-1, 36-1, 50-1, 53-2, 63-1, 73, 81-1, 95, 96, 99-1, 101-1, 128, 133, 143-2, 144-2, 174, 175-2, 207, 234-3
Alton Hughes: 218-1
Institute of Texan Cultures: 2, 3, 21-3
Kenneth Ragsdale: 200
Texas State Historical Commission: 109-1, 109-2
Texas State Library: 31, 47-1, 94-2, 100, 111, 136, 140-3, 142-2, 178-2, 221, 224
U.S. Army: 16-1, 18-1, 19-2
Rosa Lee Wylie: 220-2